THE FINANCIAL
ADVISOR
TO BUILDING
WEALTH

FROM FINANCIAL CRISIS TO FINANCIAL FREEDOM

Thomas Herold

The Financial Advisor to Building Wealth

From Financial Crisis to Financial Freedom

Revision 1.5

Thomas Herold
Evolving Wealth, LLC.

www.evolvingwealth.org

Table of Contents

<u>INTRODUCTION</u>

"Pursuing Prosperity with Financial Education"

Welcome to the Financial Advisor to Building Your Wealth

It's my pleasure to present the first edition of our quarterly publication 'Financial Advisor to Building Wealth'.

Just take a moment and think about what wealth means to you. If you're like most folk, you think it's all about money. It was for me too, until I decided to explore the topic more deeply and really consider what makes us wealthy, prosperous people. Wealth, for me, is not merely material possessions: it's your health, your lifestyle and relationships, even your mental abilities.

Curious yet? If you still think money has anything to do with wealth, you'll be in for a big surprise when you read this issue. My main aim, and the inspiration for my website and the whole of my work, is to help you learn about finance like I did – to help you transform your life, leave the past behind and take control of your wealth. Now, you might think financial terminology is about as interesting as a bag of rice falling off a shelf in China. But these days, one of the most essential and precious gifts you can give yourself is a financial education - especially given the worldwide economic crisis we are all experiencing.

Humanity is embarking on the biggest transfer of wealth in history. You may have sensed it already, and you're right: wealth is flowing at breathtaking speeds away from the financially uneducated towards people who know about finance and, crucially, how to use that knowledge to their advantage.

The current international financial crisis is a direct outcome of government and bank interventions. It's time for us to open our eyes to this and start to protect ourselves.

You might have heard the phrase, "If you always do what you've always done, you'll always get what you've always got." There's no question that, in order to secure your future and live a life that you're in control of, you must take on the task of understanding what is happening to your hard-earned money.

Once you grasp and unravel the hidden agenda of a few powerful people, you will be able to choose and reclaim your financial freedom. At the moment, this may all sound like a conspiracy theory to you; however, the research and facts contained in this book will provide you with enough evidence that there is a plan behind all this, which right now is serving other people, not you.

You'll realize that this plan is nothing new, and that the past shows similar attempts at monetary control and failure. Learning about these will make you better able to react to the present, and start creating wealth for yourself, rather than other people.

I've structured the articles into several categories. Feel free to skip between them and simply read what interests you most. Remember: this is not a course that you're doing for anyone else. This is a gift to yourself. Read the articles that apply to you, and in doing so you will broaden your knowledge and feel more qualified to keep learning and growing your wealth.

All the articles have been taken from the Wealth Building Course website and assembled here for you to make your financial learning simpler and more convenient. I've left out several articles which focused on issues that have now been overtaken by events. The situation is constantly changing, but the articles here have been carefully selected for their continuing relevance.

Enjoy your reading and always keep learning. Allow your mind to open up to new ideas. Believe that you can change your approach to wealth, and transform your life. As Steve Jobs once said: "Stay hungry, stay foolish."

Thomas Herold

<u>INVESTING</u>

"Putting Energy to Work"

3 Reasons Why Your Home Is A Liability And Not An Asset

If you own a home, then you are likely always telling your friends who rent that having a house is a great asset in one's investment portfolio.

Real Estate agents encourage this line of thinking by asking you as a renter why would you want to rent when you can buy for roughly the same cost. Financial experts jump on board by telling you that a house is the greatest asset purchase that you will likely ever make.

All of these people are misguided in saying that a house is an asset. As Robert Kiyosaki, the author of the Rich Dad Franchise point out, for the vast majority of people who own a house, this is in fact not the case. The subsequent paragraphs discuss three reasons why your house is not an asset, contrary to what you have been told for years.

Reason #1 - The Overwhelming Majorities of Houses Take Money Out of Your Pocket

Assets do not cost more than they yield in return. But the vast majority of houses that Americans own in fact take money out of your pocket. This is money that goes out the door every month, every year, and at irregular occurrences.

The money that is spent every month includes the mortgage payment. Mortgage payments are considerable amounts of money that are leaving your bank account. They are comprised of PMI, or principal, mortgage interest, and insurance.

The principal money is the amount that is going to reduce the actual cost of the house that you agreed to pay when you purchased it. For example, if you bought the house for $200,000, then you are actually paying down this $200,000 principal a little bit every month as part of your principal component of the mortgage payment.

The Mortgage Interest is the amount that you are being charged to have this fifteen, twenty, thirty, or even forty year loan in order to buy the house in the first place. For the first half of the mortgage life, this is actually the largest component of your monthly mortgage payment. Over the life of the mortgage, you are likely repaying $400,000 or more on the $200,000 cost of the house, when the interest is factored. This is definitely taking money out of your pocket over the course of the mortgage term.

The last part of the monthly mortgage payment is insurance. Insurance has to be paid so that the lender who actually loaned you the money to buy the house is protected in case you default on your mortgage. Once again, all of these components in the monthly mortgage payment are actually taking money out of your pocket. Because of this, your house is not an asset.

Another significant amount of money goes out of your pocket on an annual basis to pay for your property taxes. This represents yet another drain that the house creates on your actual assets. Property tax payments are often included in a mortgage payment to help a person budget the amount, rather than collected all at once. Other people pay an annual sum to their country property tax collector. However it is paid, property taxes prove to be a part of the reason that your house is not an asset.

Finally, houses also take money from your accounts on an irregular basis. These bills mostly come in the form of maintenance and repair costs. Having to buy a new water heater, paint the outside of the house, replace the roof, and treat the house for termites and other pests are all further examples of money that goes out of your pocket every month, keeping a house from being an asset.

Reason #2 - By Definition, A Liability Is Not An Asset

As mentioned above, houses take far more money out of your pocket than they put it back in it. The definition of a liability is something that costs you in cash flow each month. An asset, on the other hand, is something that brings money in positive cash flow into your finances.

The exception to the one way flow of money out lies in the tax consideration benefit that you receive from having a house. Still, this amount of money is only a portion of the interest payments that you are making being taken off of your tax bill, so it does not change the fact that more money is still going out to pay for your house than is coming in as a result of it.

By simple definition of economics, the only way that a house can actually be an asset is if it is creating a positive cash flow each and every month for you. Is your house bringing money in, or taking it out?

Reason #3 - Assets Create Positive Cash Flow Money, Putting Money In Your Pocket

The only people who can honestly say that a house is an asset for them are some of the people who are deriving rental income from their house. But just because rental income is paid every month, this does not automatically make the house an asset.

You have to line up all of the costs associated with this house and reference those against the income that is generated in the rental payments to figure it out. This is called a cash flow statement. For example, if you pay $1,500 for a monthly mortgage payment but only receive $1,200 per month in rent on the property, then this house is still a liability and not an asset. The mortgage takes away more money every month then the rent brings in.

Let's assume for a minute that your mortgage payment was only $1,200 per month while you realize $1,300 per month in rental income from the property. At first glance, this appears to be a positive cash flow. But you have to consider more than just the expenses of monthly mortgage payments. If you pay a rental agency to manage the property for you, this incurs cash outflows every month too. These may exceed the $100 positive balance between the rental income and the mortgage payment outflow.

There are other costs associated with maintaining a rental property. These include maintenance and upkeep. You have to pay for the plumber, electrician, or handy man to come and work on any failures in the house's plumbing, electrical systems, or appliances breaking down. Some people who rent out a house also pay for a monthly maintenance plan agreement that will take care of any repair costs associated with an appliance's needed repair or replacement. These costs must also be tallied in the outflow column of the cash flow statement.

Even if this leaves a slightly positive income versus expenses balance in the house's income statement, there are other financial costs and considerations. How much will it cost if one of your renters defaults on his rent for one or more months, or is forced to move out, leaving you without a renter and the associated rental income for potentially several months?

What if a renter trashes the house as he or she is leaving? These costs can be vague and fairly intangible. But they still must be included. You begin to see why even a rental property house is seldom an asset for a person, but is instead more commonly a liability, as are the overwhelming majority of houses in America.

Now is the Time to Invest in Gold and Silver

Is now a good time to make a gold investment or a silver investment? The gold price and the silver price have both risen steadily, and rather dramatically, from 2005 to the present.

Has this rise run its course or is it merely a beginning? These important questions deserves honest consideration. The following information shows why great upward pressure remains on gold and silver prices, making possible even more dramatic increases.

Some History of Gold and Silver Prices

From 1792 to 1933, the gold price was $20.67 per ounce in the United States all money could be exchanged for gold. In 1933, the US went off this gold standard, devalued the dollar to $35 per ounce of Gold, and forbade any US citizen from holding or owning any gold. Foreign citizens and banks could, however, convert their US notes into gold . After World War II, the gold-backed US dollar became the world's key currency for several reasons:

- Do I always feel as though I am behind in my work?
- Do I want myself and my team to be more productive?
- Do I need to find a balance between work and home?
- Do my team members shirk from responsibility?
- Do I struggle with distractions?

- Do I work for a business with frequent turnaround of employees?

In 1971, the dollar became fiat money; the dollar became merely a paper note having neither value in itself nor backing in real assets. This happened when President Nixon ended the ability of foreign banks to convert their US dollars into gold. Nixon's action eliminated the official $35 per ounce price of gold. The value of gold and the value of the dollar were no longer linked.

The private market, which in 1968 was allowed to set a separate price for gold, then determined the world's only gold price. At the time of Nixon's order, the gold price had recently risen to about $40 per ounce and the silver price was about $1.40 per ounce. (The market quoted gold and silver prices in US dollars per ounce.)

Since 1971, the value of the fiat dollar lay in the US government's declaration that the dollar is legal money to exchange for goods and services. The US Treasury could then pay its bills and its debts in fiat dollars. Standing behind the national debt has been the increasingly shaky assurance that the US government, or rather the US taxpayer, is good for every dollar that is owed. Still, for almost 40 years, the dollar has remained the world's currency standard largely because of the past strength and continuing importance of the US economy.

After the dollar had become fiat money, gold and silver prices increased modestly at first. But by the end of 1974, when the right of US citizens to own gold was finally restored, the price of gold had risen above $180 per ounce and the price of silver above $4.00 per ounce.

As precious metals and former currency standards, gold and silver prices almost always rise and fall together. What factors affect their price? Is now the time to make a profitable gold or a silver investment?

Yes, now is a great time for a gold or silver investment. The US and the world are on the brink of changes that could heighten economic uncertainty, and even produce fear. Of course, no one can predict any future price, but such uncertainty increases the demand for gold and silver and drives their prices up.

Spikes in Gold and Silver Prices Since 1971

Unusual or extreme conditions existed during three times when the price of gold and silver rose abnormally high. These factors often accompany economic uncertainty and higher gold prices.

1973-1975: Troubling the nation and world were the Watergate scandal, President Nixon's resignation, and Arab members taking control of OPEC and cutting oil production. Inflation was high and spiked to over 12%. The rise in the gold coincided with consumer confidence plummeting to an historic low. Additionally, gold climbed and fell nearly in tandem with both inflation and the unemployment rate, which reached 9%. Interest rates also surged to a post-war high of 12% just months before gold peaked at nearly $200 an ounce.

All of 1980: This was the year of the Iran hostage crisis. Gold and interest rates were both extremely high and extremely volatile. The price of gold skyrocketed to $850 per ounce, dropped to $485, and surged again to $710 before dropping again. Interest rates followed gold by a few months in rising to 20%, falling to 11%, and climbing back to 21% by year's end.

Consumer confidence plunged briefly and the inflation rate grew to over 14%; it was higher than 11% for nearly two years.

1982,83: Consumer confidence was very low for a prolonged period, likely caused by the highest unemployment rates since the great depression and a very high interest rates, still over 16% when gold began its rise from $296 per ounce. Inflation, however, had dropped below 7% and continued to drop as the gold price stayed between $395 and $510 per ounce.

Other Factors Affecting the Price of Gold

Deficit Spending:

Long term budget deficits decrease a country's economic stability.

Debasing the Currency:

When a nation borrows money or increases its (fiat) money supply by printing, the value of its currency decreases. Gold, however, maintains its value. Thus, when the dollar loses value, the price of gold generally increases and vice versa.

Uncertain Conditions Today:

From 1988 through the end of 2001, through the market crash of 2000 and even 9/11, the price of gradually gold fell while the dollar's value was erratic until 1995 when it increased dramatically. Unemployment, inflation, and interest rates were all low and produced the feeling of economic stability.

In January 2002, the price of gold began its rise from $280 per ounce to over $900 per ounce in 2008. During that time, the inflation rate, the interest rate, and the unemployment rate all remained low, while deficit spending and borrowing increased. Uncertainty began to build because of the wars in Afghanistan and Iraq. Gold prices seemed to rise and fall with the conditions in the Middle East, rising with the deterioration in 2006 & 2007 and falling in 2008 with the improvement in Iraq.

Dire economic conditions built up across the globe throughout 2008 and gold began a steep rise to its current price near $1200 per ounce. There are many reasons for that. Unemployment rose and stayed high. Deficit spending, debt, and money supply increases hurt currencies and economies. While gold prices are most affected by the stability of the US economy, deep weaknesses in the Euro and in many European economies have contributed to the current uncertainty.

Unfortunately, the economic uncertainty is likely to increase and put even more upward pressure on gold and silver prices. A gold investment or a silver investment could now be highly profitable for several reasons.

- The European countries involved in WWII were heavily in debt to the US.
- The US economy was very strong and the value of dollar had appreciated.
- Of all the major world currencies, only the US dollar was backed by gold.
- The US agreed to link the dollar to the gold price of $35 per ounce and exchange gold bullion for dollars.

Of course, none of these events are desired. Yet, with eyes open, the wise person will be prepared and the wise investor will seriously consider purchasing gold and silver.

Why The Precious Metals Market Will Be The Next Bubble

Michael Maloney's Rich Dad's Advisors: Guide to Investing In Gold and Silver: Protect Your Financial Future is filled with US economic history, information on how the government influences our market and economy, and advice on taking control of your own economic future without having to depend on third parties for economic security. Maloney is an expert in the area of investing in precious metals, as well as being the founder of Gold & Silver, Inc., which speaks to his knowledge and experience in the industry.

The book starts out with the premise that eventually the US economy will be in such bad shape that the dollar will be very near worthless, and people will again have to rely on gold and silver to shelter their wealth.

The key here, according to Maloney, is to get into the precious metals market before this downfall occurs and everyone is rushing to buy in. Such a jump on the market will, in Maloney's opinion, allow investors to get in when the getting is good, as opposed to when prices and demand are so high that only the super-rich can buy in. According to Maloney, this atmosphere could create the best investment opportunities in history.

Learning From History

Maloney begins with a brief history lesson, explaining that for hundreds of years numerous empires used a flat currency, printed money without an asset such as gold or silver to support it, which failed every single time, creating incredible upheaval in their societies and sometimes eventually led to their complete and utter downfall. The United States is now heading down the same path.

According to Maloney, since Nixon's presidency, when he took America off the gold standard, America has been dealing in fiat currency and has experienced the fluctuations of inflation and deflation.

Maloney continues to lay the framework for his reasoning with historical facts and representations; enough to support his position but not too many to run readers off or bore them enough to put the book down. He continues this substantiation all of the way through the book, giving it a real feeling of passion and well-thought-out reasoning.

Format

This book is an incredible read for those looking to expand their portfolio or to get into precious metals for the first time. It is not so tedious and complicated so as to make beginners feel in over their heads, nor does it talk down to the reader in any way. This makes the book approachable for investors of all investment levels.

The text covers a plethora of how-to information, including how and where to store precious metals after purchasing them; questions that many beginning investors have, but may not know where to turn to for answers. In addition, there is a great deal of advice on how to choose a precious metals firm, like how to tell the legitimate establishments from the shady ones.

There are some sections of the book where readers must do a little homework themselves and not just take Maloney's word at face value. For instance, Maloney discusses the value of gold and silver in terms that imply they always increase in value, which is not always the case. In another instance, he also implies that there is very little, if any, risk involved in investing in them, which is not true; the precious metals market can be very volatile, just as other investment vehicles.

But What About?

There are some topics that Maloney failed to discuss in the book, but which are very important to precious metals investors. For instance, he did not discuss the history of gold and silver prices. Maloney contends that the Consumer Price Index CPI's rigged; that is, that the government influences and controls the top American inflation indicator by creating deceptively low official CPI numbers each year.

He then continues on to discuss how precious metals are a reliable hedge against inflation, but does not explore the unpredictable nature of the connection between the price of gold and the rate of inflation.

Some independent homework on the price history of gold reveals that in the past gold prices have plummeted while CPI skyrocketed, and increasing gold prices corresponded to CPI plunges. This can make a reader wonder, even if CPI is rigged, what exactly is the correlation between inflation and gold? Is there one?

This book was a perfect opportunity for Maloney to delve further into this connection, but he did not do so, and that is a disappointment. This also makes the reader wonder if this flaw, a serious one no doubt, is present, what other areas of the book consider closer scrutiny?

Another instance where Maloney's ideas fall short is that precious metals are the best investment during times of deflation. If one really considers this argument, it would go thus: If the price of gold consistently rises during times of inflation, it should lower during times of deflation analogously.

With that in mind, that means that either gold is not a good hedge against inflation, or that it is not a wise investment during times of deflation. This reasoning seems faulty, and Maloney should have taken such an opportunity, in his discussion about precious metals favorability during times of depreciation, to explore further this concept so that his readers did not feel he was contradicting himself or that he was incorrect in his logic.

The other side of this coin is that it is important for readers to use Maloney's book as a starting point, to branch off from this book and dig deeper into the topic to find out as much information as possible. The book is not an end-all on the subject, and such instances should consider questions and inquiries, which should lead readers to other sources. The case Maloney makes for buying gold, silver, and other precious metals as part of a diversified portfolio is an important one that all investors should consider.

Conclusion

This book is a fast read packed with a great deal of useful information, especially for those looking to enter the precious metals market for the first time. The historical monetary information is a great foundation for future reading on the subject of precious metals investing, and the research done by Maloney and presented in this book is incredibly thorough.

He presents his position in a reader-friendly manner very accessible to even the most novice investor. The connections Maloney makes between our economy and a corrupt government sheds a great deal of light on why our economic state is where it is today, and he also illuminates some patterns throughout history that we can see currently playing out on our country financial stage today.

Maloney does a great job of explaining how America got here, why the fiat currency phenomena has not worked for other countries in the past, and how individuals can protect themselves from an out of control economic policy by investing in precious metals.

While there are some areas of discussion that are not as thorough as they could be, Maloney's reasoning and evidence causes the reader to think critically and look outside of his book for more answers and information to their questions. This is an incredible service to his readers, as this ensures they have the opportunity to expand their knowledge of the subject and make better-informed investors out of themselves.

How to Use Debt to Leverage Your Return on Investment

You are about to learn a powerful secret in this article, one that you may have never fully understood but have probably utilized in the past. It revolves around the concept of using debt to increase the return on your investments through leverage.

Any time that you buy a house with only a down payment, you are engaging in this miracle act of leverage, which turns out to be the almost magical way to make potentially significant amounts of money.

The Definition of Leverage

Leverage is properly defined as a method of multiplying gains and losses. Another way of saying this is that debt, when it is invested, actually multiplies returns. Borrowing money to purchase an investment proves to be an easy way to undertake leverage. Corporations and businesses engage in this type of activity all of the time.

Banks are a good example of this, as are insurance companies. Banks loan out their customers' deposits using a leverage of ten to one commonly. This means that they are able to collect interest payments on $10 million, even if they only have $1 million of money in deposits. Insurance companies do the same thing in a different way.

With the example of a $1 million cash position, they write insurance contracts whose claims would total $10 million or even $20 million. They get to collect premiums on all of these contracts, making their return much higher than if they only wrote $1 million worth of insurance contracts.

Use Leverage For Your Home Mortgage

Where you are concerned, this principle of leverage can also work to your advantage in using debt to increase the possible returns on your investments. A mortgage on a house is a primary example. If you buy a $200,000 house, then most likely you will be required to put down around ten to twenty percent, or $20,000 to $40,000, as a down payment.

Assume that your credit is really terrific and that you are able to borrow $180,000 from the bank, while only putting down $20,000. This means that you have received a leverage ratio that amounts to ten to one. Another way of saying this is that for every $20 of the house asset that you acquired, you have put in only two dollars of your own money, or equity.

In this example, should home prices start to rise, then you will make money, but not only the literal percentage increase of the underlying home prices themselves. Specifically, if home prices rise ten percent, then you have not only made ten percent in your investment. The home value increased from $200,000 to $220,000.

Since the money that you invested was only $20,000 in the first place, and the money that you owe to the bank is only $180,000, then you have actually increased your original investment from $20,000 to $40,000.

This represents an impressive 100% gain in the value of your investment. This became possible through the miracle of leveraging your investment through debt.

Leverage Formulas

The formulas for figuring out the possible gains to be made through leverage are as follows: leverage ratio equals the asset value divided by the equity. Similarly, the return on investment equals the leverage ratio multiplied by the percent change. So with a $200,000 asset value in the house example, divided by $20,000 in equity money that you put in, you arrive at a ten times leverage ratio, or ten to one.

The return is then figured out by multiplying that ten leverage ratio times the ten percent change in the value of the house. This is how the one hundred percent is arrived at in the example. Or put another, simpler way, you controlled $10 for every single dollar that you put into the house investment. That gave you a ten times profit return on the investment.

Leverage Considerations

It is important to be really careful when employing leverage, so that you do not become a victim like so many others in the housing crises of the last few years. While this leverage can work tremendously to your advantage when prices are rising, it also cuts both ways when prices of the asset in question are falling. Should the $200,000 house fall ten percent instead of going up by that amount, then the full $20,000 investment that you made has disappeared, but only on paper.

This is why patience can be required in this kind of leveraged investing. The lending institution will not call you looking for more money when the value of the house that the mortgage is based on declines. Such losses, as with the gains, are only realized when you sell the property in question. This means that you are able to ride out a property depreciation and wait for the prices to recover and go back up, just as you can choose not to sell a house that has increased in value.

The Real Power of Leveraging Mortgages

By now you have seen the power that leverage has to offer you in your investments. You can begin to understand how people were capable of making small fortunes if they were able to buy multiple houses, rent them out to pay their underlying mortgages, and then later on sell them when the property prices had appreciated significantly. For example, someone who started with a hundred thousand dollar house that he or she only put ten thousand dollars in, then found a reliable tenant to make the monthly rent payments equal to the mortgage, was gaining in more than one way.

On the one hand, the person was leveraging their investment to the tune of ten to one leverage ratio, as discussed in the above examples. At the same time, the individual was gaining equity, or additional dollar ownership in the property with every payment made. Yet the money for these monthly mortgage payments was coming from the rent money paid in by the tenant.

On top of this, the owner of the house received special tax write offs on the mortgage interest paid to the bank. You can do this yourself to great effect, and over time, you might build up a portfolio of house properties for which you have only put ten to twenty percent of the purchase price into the houses. And it is all accomplished through the power of leverage.

How to Find a Funding Source to Leverage Your Mortgage

Now, to begin using the power of leverage to your advantage, you will first have to find someone to make you a loan, or mortgage, on your first house property. Traditionally, this is the purvey of banks or savings and loans institutions. Banks are a good place to start looking for home loans or mortgages, but they are not the only such place to find them.

One choice for a person who has built up a great amount of money in his or her 401K is to arrange a loan against the 401K. This is not the same thing as withdrawing the money from the plan. With a 401K loan, you will actually have to pay back the loan, over a set amount of payments, and with interest. The rate will be considerably lower than taking out credit card cash advances, though perhaps not as low as a mortgage.

Another source of money to buy a house with is from a finance company, such as ditech.com or GreenLightLoans.com. Companies like these offer thirty year home loans for as little as 4.5% APR, or annual percentage rate.

Why You Must Consider Silver for Your Investment Portfolio

You will probably agree that everyone who believes in owning precious metals as a part of their portfolio loves gold. Of all the major precious metals, gold, platinum, and silver, silver seems to be overlooked, or even pointedly ignored, when it is time to make investment portfolio decisions. You may be able to think of a variety of reasons for why this is the case.

The most obvious of them is probably that silver's price is so much lower than gold and platinum prices. You have also heard about gold and platinum in the news almost every week, while the pundits seem to be mostly silent on the gray metal. The truth is that there are a variety of good reasons for why you should consider including silver in your investment portfolio.

Silver Is Also an Industrial Use Metal

One of the great things that you will find going for silver is that it is not in demand simply for jewelry and investment purposes, as is its bigger brother gold. While gold has limited additional uses besides these, silver offers more than simply inflation and safe haven protection. Silver is widely used in industries that grow over time, and it offers investors an economic recovery scenario based investment as one of its attractive facets.

The Thousands of Uses for Silver

Here are some good examples of how silver is tangibly useful and in industrial demand for you to consider. You would never be able to utilize your paper stock certificates to manufacture an anti bacterial agent. Your bank account balance will not develop film. Neither your treasury bonds, T-bills, money market accounts, nor certificates of deposit will be of any use in patching up electrical circuits. Yet silver is capable of doing all of these activities, and more importantly, it is an essential element in all of them.

Silver stands in contrast to all other commodities and paper investments in being useful for actually thousands of applications that serve to hold down the amount of silver circulating at any given time. You probably already have silver in your house without realizing it, since you own a computer, multiple television sets, and other forms of electronic equipment.

Besides being an integral component of these important home appliances, silver is found in your car bearings, in your batteries, and probably in any medical equipment that you needed when you last had surgery performed. Perhaps more importantly, silver is a key component in up and coming industries that are growing by leaps and bounds, such as water purification and solar energy.

Growing Industrial Demand for Silver

Assuming that the developing world and technologies continues to expand, then the critical demand for silver will only skyrocket. This means the silver that you should be holding in your hand or safe deposit box is constantly increasing in scarcity and real value. Paper investments, and even gold, may serve no practical use besides their principal investment role, but silver is literally indispensable.

Silver is Rarer than Gold

This little news flash will probably shock you, but silver is actually rarer than gold in today's world. The amount of silver produced each year is negligible in comparison to the yellow metal. Consider this for a moment. All of the above ground gold on earth can be fit inside of a cube that is sixty-seven feet on each side. That sounds like a ridiculously small amount of gold, and it is. But all of the above ground silver stock would go inside of a cube that is only forty-seven and a half feet per side.

You will also be surprised to learn that while there are about 5.2 billion troy ounces of gold available for use above ground, there are a mere 1.0 billion troy ounces of silver available above ground for the thousands of silver uses. Which metal would you rather have an investment in, gold that is higher priced and yet theoretically five times more abundant than silver, or silver that is astonishingly cheap by comparison and yet used daily in thousands of practical and growing industrial applications?

Silver Offers Greater Appreciation Potential Compared to Its All Time High

Gold has vaulted above its previous all time high of about $850 per ounce made back in 1980. You may have heard that it is currently trading at only a few dollars below its latest all time high of around $1,260 per ounce. Contrast this with silver. Silver reached over $42 per ounce in the early 1980's. It is under $19.50 per ounce these days.

So while gold has already eclipsed its multi-year highs and is trading just under its all time highs, silver is still $22.50 below its all time high, representing a possible in excess of one hundred and fifteen percent gain potential to reach its all time high again.

However you look at the numbers, silver possess far more room for appreciation without having to break new ground to achieve it.

Silver Features Greater Price Volatility

When you look at the daily price charts of silver versus gold over any given period of time, you will find that silver has practically always proven to be more volatile than the other precious metals. More than this, silver creates higher returns than does gold. The reasons for this are based once again on silver being considerably rarer than gold.

Such a small amount of silver throughout the world changes hands on a daily basis that even tiny amounts of silver being bought are able to significantly influence the entire silver market. Silver is one of those rare investment opportunities that showcases its volatility as a positive element. Just look at the history of the prices of silver, and you will quickly discover that silver is able to move up fast, sometimes as much as ten to twenty percent in only a short couple of weeks.

Silver Is Recommended by Savvy Self Made Billionaire Commodities' Investor Jim Rogers

Years ago, you may have heard about how George Soros and his then partner Jim Rogers made literally billions of dollars for themselves in the early 1990's in their foreign exchange investments by taking the opposite position as the Bank of England on the future of British Pounds. After they two parted ways, Jim Rogers later went on to become a legendary commodities investor based in Singapore. Jim's advice is eagerly sought out by numerous investors around the world.

In a recent interview this summer, the commodities guru was asked about his positions and sense on gold bullion investments and prices. He promptly replied that he was not selling his gold, and that he never sells gold; but that he was not buying anymore of it at these price levels. Instead, Jim said that he is buying silver aggressively now.

In his explanation for this investment behavior, he cited the fact that silver is so far below its historic all time high price. He also mentioned briefly the rarity of it when compared to gold, as well as its many industrial uses. So now you know as much about the reasons for adding silver to your investment portfolio as one of the world's richest and most successful investors of all time.

Gold In Your Portfolio Will Protect You From Hyperinflation

If you have been watching the news or financial television at all over the last couple of years, then you will know that gold is in the middle of a long running bullion market that shows no signs of letting up any time soon. So far for 2010, gold prices have increased by an impressive ten percent for the year, setting them up for a tenth consecutive yearly advance.

This represents the longest running winning gold streak since back in 1920, as investors continue to pile into the investment vehicle that has historically protected their wealth from economic turbulence and the likelihood of continued currency debasement. With gold up from $250 to $1,250 per ounce since 2001, an astonishing four hundred percent rise in that time, you might agree with some investors that the best gains for gold lie in the past already. The following paragraphs go through a number of the best reasons for investing in gold today.

Projections for Gold

Although gold prices may already seem high compared to their previous high set in 1980 at around $850 per ounce, this is not really the case. The inflation adjusted 1980 gold high represents around $2,750 per ounce in today's dollars.

Using this basis for gold prices, you can see that gold per ounce prices may still have another $1,500 to go before they reach their true value all time high.

Projections for the future price of gold run all over the board, though the vast majority of respected opinions tend towards higher prices in the near future. The recent August forecast for median gold price suggested by twenty-nine different gold traders, analysts, and investors surveyed by the respected Bloomberg calls for $1,500 per ounce by next year.

Deutsche Bank, the world's largest foreign currency trading operation, looks for $1,550 per ounce this coming year. Barclays, the world's largest ETF and commodities trading investment bank, forecasts that gold prices will break through first $1,350 per ounce then $1,600 per ounce before the end of 2010. Jim Sinclair, a long time godfather in the gold trading business, has his sights for gold set on $1,650 per ounce before the end of 2011.

Citigroup, among the largest banks on earth, looks for $2,000 per ounce or higher in the next two to three years. These price projections are mostly based on rising gold demand, falling gold supplies and mine output, and the long term decline in reliable gold production. With so many widely ranging estimates for the prices of gold, you will likely wonder what is the basis for all of these wild seeming projections.

The Move Towards A Global Currency

Among the greatest positive elements for gold these days is the move away from using the U.S. dollar as the global reserve currency.

Since the Euro has not yet been fully accepted as its replacement, central banks from the world's wealthier nations are looking for some other reliable place to park their foreign exchange reserves.

Gold has made major strides towards becoming that replacement global currency. As various central banks and these nation's governments have looked for solid investments that they can utilize to back up their riskier investments, as well as sometimes fragile paper currencies, gold has come out on top in many of the central banking decisions. China has long been known to be quietly increasing its strategic gold holdings and reserves in an effort to make its Yuan a major world currency.

You may have been surprised, as was much of the world last year, when India announced that it would acquire an enormous two hundred tons of gold in 2009. The island nations of Sri Lanka and The Seychelles made similar announcements on a much smaller scale following India's big splash. Expect to see an increasing number of these kinds of announcements regarding central banks and gold purchases going forward.

Gold Has Intrinsic Value

If you are still a skeptic as to why you should buy gold at today's prices, then consider something. In the last few years, the world has watched as historic and respected financial institutions, such as Lehman Brothers, Bear Stearns, Washington Mutual, and the world's largest insurance company AIG, collapsed within days to weeks.

Other major multinational financial firms with hundreds of years of history, like the Royal Bank of Scotland and Merrill Lynch, once the world's largest brokerage house, were only saved by multiple billion dollar bailouts from governments or by buyouts from rivals. Institutions and promises that once seemed rock solid suddenly became clearly ethereal.

In the new economic reality that has emerged following the financial collapse of 2008 and the Great Recession, investments that actually have intrinsic value suddenly look more appealing to you. What you may not know is that gold is perhaps the greatest embodiment of intrinsic value. For literally thousands of years, it has proven its utility and demonstrated its worth again and again. It has represented both a means of exchange and currency throughout the growth and fall of every regional and world empire. Gold has never completely collapsed or gone bankrupt, and since it is not tied to any individual company or government, it can not.

You Can See and Touch Your Gold Investment

With gold bars or coins, you are actually able to see, feel, and touch your precious investment. Stocks, bonds, and mutual funds are all representations of a company or government and its promises. Other people make those decisions that influence the value of all of these other types of investments.

When you own gold, you can be sure that you have an actual valuable metal, not a piece of paper that is backed up by a possibly shaky bank, nor a complex derivative investment that may or may not be actually guaranteed by the company that created it when their chips are down. And while no country, along with its accompanying currency or bonds, has ever lasted forever, gold has been with us since the beginning of time.

Rarity of Gold and It's Tiny Market

Another reason why you should have confidence in investing in gold today lies in the small amount of it that is literally available. It is not an exaggeration when you hear that all of the gold above ground in the world today would fit into a box that is 22.3 feet long on each of its sides.

To show you how little gold is actually produced every year, the London Bullion Association trades the whole year's mining production of gold in only four to five days trading. Only .087 billion ounces of gold are mined in an entire year. In fact, if only a few percentage points worth of the money in the U.S. stock markets moved into gold in a short amount of time, then gold prices would be forced up to around $5,000 by the increased demand and truly limited available supply.

Protection Against Inflation

Among the biggest motivating factors for buying gold has always revolved around the fears of inflation. In the last four years alone, between the combined printing press efforts of the Treasury and the Federal Reserve, you have watched as the supply of existing U.S. dollars in the world has been increased by more than three hundred percent. One day soon, this lurking specter of inflation will rear its ugly head.

Some experts have even said that you will possibly see hyperinflation in the United States within the next one to two years as a result of all of this American currency debasing activity that has been going on. Should that dreadful day finally come, then it will not be your stocks, bonds, and mutual funds that save you from the financial storm, but your portfolio of gold holdings.

Why The Next Financial Crash Will Be The Bond Market

Have you ever stopped to consider what the largest investment market is in the United States? If you said the stock market, then you are wrong by a long shot.

The correct answer is the bond market. The bond markets are so much larger than the stock markets as if the stock markets were only a few drops in the bond market's proverbial bucket.

Bond markets have long been held as sacrosanct, considered by most people to be far safer than the stock markets. The unfortunate truth is that the bond markets are likely to be where the next crash occurs.

If this in fact proves to be the case, then it will be catastrophic for you personally, as well as for everyone who is heavily invested in bonds, especially for fixed income retirees who depend on these investments to survive. In the following paragraphs, you will read the disturbing reasons why the bond market is likely to be the next shoe to drop in the continuously unfolding economic crisis begun in the Great Recession.

Background for The Possible Fall of the Bond Markets

Many of you will no doubt shake your heads at this assessment advanced by Robert Kiyosaki. You wonder how it is possible that the U.S. bond markets could be sick and worsening in their condition by the day. The answer to this troubling question goes back to 1971.

It was in this year that you saw the U.S. led by then President Richard Nixon abandon the gold standard. The dollar ceased almost immediately to be an instrument backed by tangible value. Instead, it became an instrument backed up only by debt and the world's faith in the ability of the American tax payer to repay the increasingly growing obligations.

These debt obligations have only increased in time until the year 2007. At this point, thanks to the arrival of the Great Recession and the monumental financial collapse, the American debt level jumped exponentially, going from a matter of only billions to more than fourteen trillion dollars in forty years.

It has become so bad that in mid May of this year, you actually heard Moody's Investor Service come out and claim that the venerable United States government may soon see its much envied AAA credit rating, and that of the U.S. Treasury bonds, tested for the first time in the American century that began following World War I. This is no laughing matter.

A First Bond Market Downgrade

Moody's will not be the first significant ratings agency in the world to downgrade the U.S. debt and bonds. You might wonder how anyone can know this.

The answer is because the premier Chinese bond rating agency, Dagong Global Credit Rating Company, has already done this.

In late July of this year, Dagong dropped its AA+ rating of the U.S bonds and credit worthiness one notch down to AA. That still ranks above its opinions of Germany and Japan, which it holds at AA-, but it came along with a negative outlook remark. This signifies that they intend to downgrade U.S. debt even further in the coming months.

Why the Dagong Global Credit Rating Matters

You are possibly rolling your eyes at the news that a Chinese rating agency is the one that downgraded U.S. debt and bonds. This is not Moody's, S&P, or Fitch after all, you say. Why should it matter at all what the Chinese think about the U.S. bond markets?

The disturbing response is that the Chinese are the world's largest buyers of U.S. sovereign debt, better known as Treasury bonds. The value of American government bonds is dependent on more demand constantly appearing in the bond markets. Someone has to buy these new bonds to hold up the prices. This is because of the fact that the U.S. continues to issue new supply.

The Growing Supply and Demand Problem with U.S. Bonds

As supply in anything increases, and demand does not keep up pace with the mounting supply, then prices have no where to go but down, according to the law of supply and demand. This is why the increase in government spending that has only exponentially increased under the present administration is such a dangerous problem.

Government revenues are falling. This means that all of the new spending has to be paid for from increased amounts of debt. So more and more treasury bonds are being created and floated in order to finance the debt spending. It represents a ticking time bomb of disastrous proportions.

The Bond Market Crash Impact on Bond Holders

The possible resulting collapse of U.S. bonds will be especially bad for the holders of U.S. Treasury bonds. Countless American corporations and banks hold these, believing them to be guaranteed. Fixed income retirees collect these in their retirement portfolios, believing them to be supremely safe. Once they were. But if you see the bond market crash as a result of U.S. government debt downgrades, these IOU pieces of paper also known as Treasury bonds will become pariah.

Plummeting bond prices will be devastating for the retirees who depend on the income from these instruments and the gradual sales of them to finance their retirements. Banks have only recently come off of their sub prime real estate collapse and defaults too.

Imagine them having to now weather a severe deterioration in what they up till now believed to be their most trustworthy assets. The consequential damage to the U.S. financial system will be catastrophic. You thought bank failures in the hundreds were bad. Imagine closing banks by the thousands. If the bond market crashes, this will only be one of the unfortunate results.

The Bond Market Crash Impact on All Americans

As bad as bankrupt retirees and rapidly failing banks sound, this is only the tip of the iceberg for the way that average middle class Americans will be affected by the collapsing bond market. You might not be immediately clear on why this would be the case. Your average American middle class person is not holding significant quantities of U.S. Treasury Bonds, after all.

The relationship between Treasury Bond prices and rates are inversely related. Because treasury bond prices are high and stable, the government, and hence all Americans, are able to borrow money for ridiculously low interest rates. The government only has to pay between zero and point twenty-five percent interest on its massive debt now. But if the bond market prices plummet with the lack of demand to keep up with supply, the the interest rates will move the other direction, sharply higher.

You might wonder how much higher they could go. A sudden precipitous plunge in U.S. Treasury bond prices could send interest rates up to double digits, according to some economists. The effects of this would be devastating and widespread in their immediate impact. In order to fight inflation, the rising costs of goods and services, as foreign investors fled the U.S. Treasuries market altogether, the Fed would be forced to raise interest rates to match.

This would be necessary not only to fight off a sudden surge in inflation, but also a potentially crashing dollar value. The resulting rates that you pay for every form of debt, from cars to credit cards, to home mortgages, would skyrocket. Government services would have to be drastically reduced, as Washington was forced to spend the majority of its annual income on servicing the debt at the much higher interest rates.

This is not as far fetched as it might seem. Both the financial editor of the prestigious Financial Times of London and the former head of the IMF have painted this scenario as a specter likely to face the U.S. and its tax paying citizens in the near future.

Why Silver Is The New Gold

Recently investment experts Mike Maloney and David Morgan took part in the first ever Silver Summit Asia event in Singapore. Check out the clip below with some of Mike and David 's latest thoughts on silver's bright future:

Why Silver?

Most of the gold that has ever been mined is still with us today; perhaps 90% according to some analysts. The opposite is true for silver. Silver is used heavily by industrial demand, it is estimated that 90% of all the silver mined in the past 5,000 years has been used up, thrown away, unrecoverable.

Epithermal Deposits - a geological term upholding the idea that most of the silver ore deposits in the Earth's crust were deposited at shallow depths, near the surface. Most of the easy silver finds have already been made, easy silver production projects are next to nonexistent today!

Disappearing Supply

Every year that goes by, more silver is used worldwide than is being mined and recovered by recycling.

Current world silver demand runs at 900 million ounces a year. Current world mining rates of production stand at 600 million ounces annually.

Over the next 25 years the world will need approximately 15 billion ounces of silver to meet current demand. The US Geological Survey projects the earth may contain only 8.5 to 18 billion ounces remaining in its crust.

It's going, going, almost gone!

Today US silver production runs at roughly 40 million ounces a year. Over the past few years, silver production in the United States is down nearly 30%. Nevada, formerly the largest mining state for silver has seen its silver production decline by more than 50% over the past five years. Many silver ore bodies in the United States are running dry.

Silver Eagles are Maxing Out

In 2007, just over 9 million Silver Eagle coins were struck and sold to the public. In 2008, the figure more than doubled to 20.5 million coins sold. Last year the US Mint witnessed another large increase in demand as investors scooped 30.4 million Silver Eagles. Thus far in 2010 alone, almost 12 million Silver Eagles have been sold to the public!

Silver Eagle coins by law, are to be comprised of newly mined silver obtained from domestic sources, meaning the coins are to consist of silver newly mined (within a 12 month time frame) in the United States only.

Taking this into account, we would like to again call your attention to the ever-increasing demand for Silver Eagles, below is a chart of the latest updates for 2010 Silver Eagle sales thus far:

If we extrapolate the data above, investor demand is on pace for more than 35,000,000 Silver Eagles to be struck and sold this year alone. Again, here in the USA we mine roughly 40 million ounces of silver annually, this means we are on pace to use almost 90% of this years domestic silver production for Silver Eagle demand alone!

What will happen when Silver Eagle demand outstrips supply? Will the minting laws be changed? Will they merely raise the premiums? The public is hardly aware yet Silver Eagle sales are reaching their legal supply threshold.

It is our firm belief we are in the midst of the great Gold and Silver rush of the 21st Century. In the coming wild years ahead, shortages of physical silver and gold will become the norm, not the exception. Those who hold physical bullion should greatly benefit.

So why is Silver the New Gold?

There is less silver in the world for investors today than gold. In the western world we take silver for granted, we are befuddled to believe that silver is common and easy to obtain. For many regions of the world this is not the case. Many of our Asian-Pacific customers have expressed to us that they have no trouble buying gold bullion in their countries, but finding investment grade silver is next to impossible.

Silver cannot be substituted; it has too many unique properties. Nothing conducts electricity or heat as well as silver. No metal is a better reflector of light. Silver is integral in the photographic process and has important health benefits. The white metal is an absolute necessity in high tech as every server, cell phone, monitor, computer, and electric switch. It's in your TV, washing machine, refrigerator, batteries, DVD's, iPod, wall switches, and mirrors. Without silver our modern way of life is impossible!

Silver's Newest Innovative Uses?

Here are some of the latest uses:

- Do I always feel as though I am behind in my work?
- Do I want myself and my team to be more productive?
- Do I need to find a balance between work and home?
- Do my team members shirk from responsibility?
- Do I struggle with distractions?
- Do I work for a business with frequent turnaround of employees?

Bottom Line?

Silver is absolutely necessary for our modern way of life. Silver is also a necessity to hedge against the rampant fiat currency expansion going on all over the world. We are running out of silver and there is no end to the inflationary threats central banks are educing upon us!

As Mike says, "Silver is cheaper than dirt right now!", and the best news of all is that you are one of the very few people in the world who understands this along with the opportunity to take advantage.

Outperform The Stock Market with the Greenblatt Formula

Four and a half years ago, an amazing pocket sized primer came out on telling you the secrets for outperforming the stock market in any year, be it good, bad, or ugly. The Little Book That Still Beats the Market, written by Joel Greenblatt, offers you what other numerous volumes have failed to do for years.

It makes the sometimes complex subject of investing successfully so understandable that even a grade school student can figure it out and do well at it. His new and updated version of the book that recently came out is entitled The Little Book That Still Beats The Market.

About the Author Joel Greenblatt

Joel Greenblatt, the author of The Little Book that Still Beats the Market, is an adjunct professor at Colombia Business School. Along with this, he has been the Founder, as well as Managing Partner, of his private investment partnership Gotham Capital. This fund has managed an astonishing average annual investment return of forty percent for in excess of twenty years. His impressive credentials are sure to have your attention right away.

Goal of The Little Book That Still Beats The Market

Joel Rosenblatt's goal in writing this book was astonishingly simple. He wanted to create a work that could effectively explain to his five children how to become successful stock market investors. His children were aged six to fifteen when he wrote the first edition. His first work was called a wild success, greatly exceeding his own expectations.

Background of The Little Book that Still Beats the Market

You probably have heard the saying that two years as a student in an MBA program at business school will not show you the means of more than doubling the stock market's return. It is said that two hours with The Little Book that Still Beats the Market will. That is all of the time that you need to read the entire primer for doubling stock market returns.

Joel Rosenblatt's 2005 original Little Book That Beats The Market sold more than three hundred thousand copies and has already earned a place as among the classic must reads of finance literature. In this first work, the author showed you the way that you can simply outperform the best known market averages through using an easy and systematic approach.

This approach centers around Joel's formula that looks for solid businesses as they are offered at on sale prices. Joel used this formula over a period from 1988 to 2004 to create and routinely update a portfolio of thirty different stocks that had the highest combined rankings.

His results, which he shared in the first book, proved to be amazing. He had only a single down year in that time period. More than this, his magic formula portfolio returned over thirty percent per year versus the twelve and a half percent yearly return for the S&P500 over the same time frame.

Synopsis of The Little Book that Still Beats the Market

His update The Little Book That Still Beats the Market comes out on the heels of the worst years in recent stock market history. In this new version, Joel Greenblatt expands upon the prior research and updates the original version's findings. He now offers you both data and his analysis that includes the financial crisis of the last few years, along with his model portfolio's actual performance running until the end of 2009.

In Greenblatt's characteristically easy to understand and highly readable style, he goes through the basic, central tenets of investing successfully in the stock market. More than this, Rosenblatt actually shares his formula that has been tested over time. This formula simply involves purchasing companies that are better than the average at prices that are lower than the average stock price. Best of all, it makes it an automatic process.

Perhaps what is most impressive about Rosenblatt's formula is that it is considered to be a true breakthrough phenomenon in the professional investing world. Yet despite this accomplishment, Joel is able to share it and clearly explain it to you by only employing a sixth grade student's level of math and simple language that anyone can understand. He also uses a good bit of humor to make it a more fun reading experience.

The authors shares with you how you can employ his brain child formula in order to surpass professional money managers and the stock market average by significant amounts. On top of this, Rosenblatt details the reasons that practically all individual as well as professional investors miss out on consistent success. He finally shares why his formula will continue to work for you and anyone else using it long after everyone is aware of it and how it works.

The Reason Why The Formula Works

The formula itself is proven to be simple in Joel Rosenblatt's ground breaking book. Comprehending why it works so well is the main component of success for those of you who read the book and take it to heart. The tiny book actually brings you along on a one step at a time journey of discovery to learn the main concepts of value investing.

It does this in such a method that you are able to believe in the longer term time frame necessary for the process to work. The author tells you that it is no good following the formula if you will not have the courage and confidence to stay with it in both good and bad times in the markets.

Joel Rosenblatt stands almost alone in saying that an average investor can outperform the stock markets over the longer term time frame. Thanks to his value approach formula that finds good companies that are bargains as their share price is inexpensive compared to the company's profitability, practically any one can do this. You see why this formula works, but you need to understand how it works specifically as well.

How the Formula Works

The whole key to the author's wildly successful work is the formula itself. Stocks in Greenblatt's formula are ranked based on only two variables. These are the earnings yield, or percentage of earnings over stock price, and the company's return on their capital, or percentage of profits made measured against their capital employed.

These two numbers are plugged in for a wide variety of companies to come up with his model portfolio of thirty stocks at a time. The book is full of statistics and other proofs of the success of this magic formula. Yet, in the end, Joel talks up your faith component that will be necessary to help you to wade through the short term market down periods. In the end, he says it is your faith in the unarguable logic of his magic formula that will ensure that the formula really works out for you over the longer time frame.

Other Ideas in The Little Book That Still Beats the Market

Joel Rosenblatt also goes through an elementary education explanation of the main concepts of investing. These include return, risk, interest, and business valuation. By the time you finish going through the two hour easy read, you too will be ready to tackle the commonly touted as too complex world of successful stock market investing.

In the end, Rosenblatt's ideas and magic formula are really only a slightly different take on the mainstream concepts of value investing. This is undoubtedly part of their appeal, as well as reason for why they work so effectively.

Why Investing in More Paper Assets is Not Diversifying

You have likely talked with more than one financial adviser in your life time. One thing that you may not have realized when you compared the different ideas of these various investment advisers is that they are basically all recommending the same idea, just in slight variations and with different words.

The overwhelming majority of these investment professionals will claim that you should more or less divide your investments up between stocks, bonds, mutual funds, and cash instruments. They will call this diversifying your portfolio to reduce the risk. If you dig deeper though, you will discover that investing in more paper assets, such as stocks, bonds, and mutual funds, does not actually turn out to be truly diversifying your portfolio.

The Concept of Diversification Explained

When financial people tell you about diversification, they are discussing the ways to reduce your risk through investing in a range of different assets. You are supposed to benefit from this because well diversified portfolios actually contain a smaller amount of risk than those that are invested into only one type of investment or asset class.

If you are at all a risk intolerant investor, then you will want to do at least some diversification. People who are especially fearful of risk and economic uncertainty will engage in a greater amount of diversification.

Examples of Mainstream Diversification

There is an age old adage that warns you against putting all of your proverbial eggs into only one basket. This is because if you drop the basket, then all of the eggs will likely break. By putting all of your eggs into separate baskets, then you will greatly reduce the risk of breaking, or losing, all of them, even though one or two could break and become lost.

An un-diversified type of portfolio would be one that contains only a single company's stock. In case you do not know, this is extremely risky, since individual stocks can easily fall by as much as half in a single year. In the last several years, you have watched as blue chip financial company stocks fell all the way to even zero.

Financial experts will tell you that a portfolio comprised of twenty different stocks is far less likely to drop by fifty percent. This is particularly the case if you select all of these stocks from differing industries, types, and sizes of companies. An even better way for you to diversify, per mainstream financial advisers, is to purchase stocks that are based on companies headquartered in other countries.

They might also suggest other types of investments like mutual funds, bonds, or money market funds. There is a problem with this advice as it pertains to diversifying your portfolio, since all of these different types of assets still have an underlying theme in common.

The Commonality of Paper Assets

The biggest problem with calling the purchasing of different kinds of stocks, bonds, mutual funds, treasury bills, and even money markets and certificates of deposit diversifying is that all of these different investments possess at least a few things in common. Remember the idea behind true diversification is to get into investments that are inherently different from one another. What makes all of these differing investment ideas ultimately similar?

It is the fact that they are all paper assets, whose value is also expressed in another paper asset, that of the dollar or a competing national currency. For example, a bond is simply a promise on paper from a company to repay money that you loaned to it to fund its ongoing operations or expansion plans. Treasury Bills are the same concept, with the borrower being the United States Federal Government, instead of a mere corporation.

Even certificates and money market funds are still paper based promises from banks and lending institutions to repay you money that you loan them so that they can make loans to still other people. A stock is even less secure than are these other types of investments, since stocks do not promise you anything. Ultimately, a share of a stock represents only the confidence held in a company by its investors. Confidence can be a very shaky and shifting concept in the end, easily destroyed by a rumor or bit of bad news.

The fact of the matter that you must grasp is that all of these paper based investments are more or less the same in the end, only different flavors of the same dessert. They are all based on merely promises or confidence in a company, bank, or even government. As such they can all be upended relatively quickly and easily, in particular in an unstable and evolving world like the one today.

The Common Underlying Currency of Paper Assets

You heard another commonality to all of these types of paper assets hinted at above. They are mostly all tied to the value of a single sovereign currency, like the United States dollar. No one is laughing anymore when the former head of the IMF and the financial editor of the London Times make repeated and persistent claims that the viability, stability, and even value of the U.S. dollar can not be taken for granted in the wake of the Great Recession.

In a very real sense, the United States has become a much larger version of Greece, where the amount of debt to government income level is no laughing matter. Is an actual run on the U.S. dollar in the cards, or even possible, as has been suggested by reputable individuals in the last months and year? The principal of diversification would tell you that if there is even a remote chance of a U.S. default on its sovereign debt, then you need to put a significant portion of your investment dollars into something that is not denominated in dollars.

This type of diversification would limit, or more realistically reduce, holdings of the most of cherished investments in America today. U.S. company stocks, bonds, mutual funds, money market funds, certificates of deposit, bank balances, and even Treasury bills would all fall into this category in the end.

What would that leave investors like you who are eager to follow a true policy of diversification of your assets? The alternatives are explored in the following paragraphs.

What Are Non Paper Asset Classes?

You are probably wondering what types of investments are left for real diversification purposes at this point. If you are trying to diversify away from having all of your eggs in the U.S. Dollar basket, then you might look into foreign currencies or investments based in such foreign currencies as the British Pound, Eurozone Euro, Japanese Yen, or Swiss Franc.

The problem with foreign currencies, and investments based in them, is that they are still ultimately only based on the faith and trust in each of those sovereign countries. Ultimately, they are still paper assets.

Non paper assets that make for excellent diversification include tangible investments that are based on physical assets. The two biggest types of these are real estate and precious metals. Real Estate is technically not based in any one country's currency, regardless of where it is located. You can put your hands and feet on it. It is also permanent, and is not going anywhere.

The same is true of precious metals like gold, silver, and platinum. These commodities can be held in a safe deposit box in the form of coins or bars. They do not depend on any government or corporate entity's promises, credit, or credibility whatsoever. Gold and silver also have the appeal of having been accepted as money and a viable form of payment for more than five thousand years. No matter how good your favorite blue chip company is, its odds of lasting for that amount of time are practically non-existent.

MINDSET

"Changing Habits, Attitudes and Intentions"

The Hidden Forces That Shape Our Decisions

Ayn Rand, 20th-century writer and philosopher, wrote, "Rationality is man's basic virtue, the source of all his other virtues. Irrationality is a commitment to a course of blind destruction; that which is anti-mind, is anti-life." To Rand, irrationality was something to be despised, an unsolicited intruder into man's celestial nature of thought and reason. In her tightly-strung world of philosophy and thought, rational man reigns, and quirks, nuances and absurdities are mistakes to be quickly tossed.

Dan Ariely, 21st-century behavioral scientist at Duke University, writes in his seminal book, Predictable Irrational (2008), "This book is about human irrationality" about our distance from perfection. Understanding irrationality is important for our everyday actions and decisions, and for understanding how we design our environment and the choice it presents to us. Man, thinks Ariely, is not a product of rational-choice economic models; he is intrinsically volatile and emotional consistently so. He is predictably irrational.

Ariely's Purpose

In his 13-chapter book, Ariely introduces and expounds on his radically new theory of human behavior, one that replaces a man's mathematical mind with human emotion and feeling. He intends on imprinting it onto his readers as well.

Ariely declares "My goal, by the end of this book, is to help you fundamentally rethink what makes you and the people around you tick." He adds a short blurb at the end of his lofty ambition: "Once you see how certain mistakes are [repeated] again and again, I think you will begin to learn how to avoid some of them."

With these statements, and several others similar to them, Ariely is outlining the scope of his manuscript. This book is not aimed at Ph.D.'s or practicing economists this is a book for you and me, designed to wake us up and examine our lives, as Socrates would have it, from a new and sometimes slightly uncomfortable viewpoint.

Ariely isn't another run-of-the-mill, comb-over economist, he is freethinker, and seems to enjoy a neighborly scrap. Staring convention in the face, Predictably Irrational presents a new lens for viewing behavior to both marketers and buyers alike. It shakes the business and marketing industries by the hair and offers outsiders an insider's glimpse into the cogs and gears of human behavior. Anyone with an interest in business, psychology, marketing, or is pursued by the question: "Why?" should read this book. It is a book for the rebels and the curious.

Bored to Tears or Up All Night?

Ariely does not dress up his theories with verbose economic-speak or wordy ivory tower explanations. His account is concise, accurate, and intelligent, but does not sacrifice accuracy or clarity. Ariely possesses that rare and yet inestimably valuable ability to convey novel ideas in a simple and interesting form. Predictably Irrational is more than an exposition - it is a fun read.

The experiments and research brimming on nearly every page only adds to the enjoyment. From Halloween trick-or-treating to poetry readings to product freebies to ahem adult entertainment, Ariely's research supports each argument against conventional economics with a gamut of experiments that turn each previous premise topsy-turvy in a hurry.

Each experiment is succinctly introduced, characters are portrayed, and the research proceeds in an orderly and simple fashion. Ariely's choice of research usually includes MIT and other Ivy League college students as participants, which can elucidate some juicy sarcasm from the reader, who gets to read about the average Joe prejudices of these elite intelligentsia.

The Science Behind the Science

In context of the larger scientific community, Ariely leads a fleet of behavioral scientists who proudly and steadfastly challenge the conventional theories of market economics. Ariely, and others like him, posit their theories as the antitheses of Adam Smith-type economists. Others, however, such as Richard B. McKenzie, Professor of Enterprise and Society at the University of California, Irvine, argue that many of the Ariely's eakthroughs are explainable at least in part by conventional economic theory. Nevertheless, McKenzie concedes people are not perfectly rational.

Thankfully, we are not faced with two extreme choices: complete, emotion-driven irrationality or precise rationality. The human being is a complex creature, and is a unique combination and not always a balanced one of logical sagacity and sentimental passion. Reality generally lays somewhere in the middle of any spectrum perhaps Predictably Irrational is no different?

Yet we should probably forgive any of Ariely's excessive praises of irrationality. As an irrational creature himself, Ariely launches himself headfirst into his exciting theories, potentially disregarding commentators like McKenzie, who calmly offer more conventional, albeit more dull, alternatives. After all, great inventors and discovers James Cook, Thomas Edison, Michael Faraday, Henry the Navigator, Marc Andreesson, Johann Gutenberg, James Watt, and more, threw themselves into their work with the same fervor and "dare we say?" pigheadedness.

Their creations, milestones in society's technological trek, oftentimes caused social chaos and wrecked economic markets. They were professionals at upsetting the balance of power. If they were wrong and many times they were they were wholly, not half-heartedly, wrong. If Ariely overstates his case, and as one who has read the proponents of both conventional economics and new approaches, I doubt that he does, he does so with scientific conviction.

A Rational Animal?

As Bertrand Russell said: man is a rational animal. All my life, I have been searching for evidence which could support this. Ariely asserts that humans, in terms of rationality, are much different than they think they are. He leads his peers in developing this salient and electrifying theory that is taking the R&D psychology department by storm: behavioral economics.

Predictably Irrational is an excellent read, an engaging thesis, and a welcome departure from normality. It's more than good science; it's a good book. And for all the doubters, take a moment to remember Martin Luther King, Jr. and William Tyndale. Or Ferdinand Magellan and Christopher Columbus. Still think the earth is flat?

Seven Keys to Financial Success That Pay Off

If you were offered a choice of a million dollars to spend in your business today or a book that taught you how to earn an extra million, which would you choose?

While the first option probably sounds tempting, by accepting the money you will likely take it for granted. You may end up wasting it on things you could probably do without, like new expensive office furniture or luxury company cars. The most successful business people know that every dollar you spend today is worth ten dollars in the future when invested properly. Therefore, the book that teaches you how to earn the money for yourself is a more worthwhile choice.

Knowledge has the power to earn you money. Obviously you and your business will be better off with the knowledge than with a quickly squandered million. Your respect and understanding for money will improve by earning the million dollars on your own. Plus, saving and investing now will reap greater rewards in the future.

To gain a better understanding of smart money management and investing to help secure the future of your business, consider the following seven keys to financial success:

Key #1: Save Ten Percent of Your Income:

This Key is the foundation of all your financial dealings. Aside from the value invested in savings, putting ten percent does three other things for you. First it makes you more confident. You won't have to worry about little money emergencies, and pride will grow from your control.

Second, having money allows you to take advantage of new business opportunities as they arise. Plus, your confidence will tend to attract more opportunities.

Third, by saving ten percent you create a cushion. This gives your business security immediately, and it provides some security in case of uncertainties in the future.

Key #2: Learn Before You Earn:

If you have no knowledge of money and investing, you will likely fear both. To gain a basic understanding, go to the library and read some books on investing and money management. These texts will give you plenty to go on. Many classes, tapes, and people exist that can help you as well, so seek them out.

Key #3: Be a Positive Thinker:

Anyone can find problems with any course of action. But negative thinking is not constructive for you or the type of successful people you want to be around. The doer focuses on the upside of situations, and if you never take action, you'll never gain success or the experience needed for success. Many times, the worst that can happen if you don't succeed is a minor setback that you can learn from.

Obviously this doesn't mean you can plunge ahead blindly. You prepare yourself first by obtaining the best advice possible. And you anticipate the problems. But then you must commit yourself to gain the benefits. Too many people let their negative thoughts scare them away from areas they can succeed in. They never get started.

Key #4: Invest in Areas You're Passionate About:

Nothing supports success like passion. If you love what you do, your passion will carry you past the rough spots. Very few of us can make success of something we don't care about. For example, if someone offered to pay your tuition to medical school, would you be willing to put forth all the effort required to succeed at it? Unless you're passionate about becoming a doctor, then probably not. Likewise, panhandlers can make over forty dollars an hour, which is far higher than average. But if you're not passionate about it, then you probably won't want to do it.

In reality, you could do hundreds of things to make money in your business. But success will be even more rewarding when you're passionate about what you're doing. So invest your time and money in something you really care about.

Key #5: If It Seems Too Good to be True, It Probably Is:

Sometimes people invest wildly because they are unrealistic, and other times scam artists and crooks are just after their money. Realize that you'll usually lose money if you invest in long shots, or if you expect to receive very high returns.

For example, playing commodities markets is a high risk endeavor. Unlike the stock market, in commodities someone loses every time someone wins. And if you invest in this "game" you will be playing against the producers and users of the commodities who have more information than you'll ever have. Day-trading is another gamble. So no matter how safe an investment opportunity or business venture sounds, if it seems too good to be true then you're probably better off turning it down.

Key #6: To Make Progress, You Have to Get Started:

Many people have good ideas or intentions, but few take action. Don't be afraid to commit yourself. Even if your start means just reading in the library, you must take action to get results.

Action makes things happen for you. The more action you take, the more you'll learn to take smarter actions next time. You will often learn more from your own mistakes than from your successes. This is how you gain experience.

Key #7: Build Your Own Habits:

Once you've found actions that work, turn them into habits. By creating a habit, routine actions become easier and you are freed up for more creative activities. Habits also make it easier for you to continue to take action even when you don't feel like it or if you hit some other barrier.

Financial Success for Your Future: Knowledge has the power to earn money, therefore understanding the keys to financial success can pay off with great rewards. When you save ten percent of your business income, you build your financial security.

By taking the time to learn the way money works, you'll be less likely to make costly mistakes. And positive thinking will give you confidence to take intelligent risks.

A passion for what you do will make your success more rewarding. But keep in mind that any business opportunity that sounds too good to be true, most likely is an unsafe venture. Then understand that to make progress, you must take action. Finally, building good money habits will make your routine activities easier and free up more time for creative endeavors.

When you learn and use these seven keys to financial success, you'll build the stability of your business and grow you earning potential as a result.

You Must Take Risks in Life to Become a Success

It's a fact that you can learn from a mistake after you admit you have made it, and that you cannot blame anyone else for your actions because you'll never learn anything from what you've done. You have to own up to your mistake and become responsible. Once you're able to admit that, you can move the focus of the blame away from others.

Making Mistakes in Modern Society

People are taught in school, in their families, or at the workplace that a mistake is something you should feel guilty about even though setbacks are inevitable and part of everyday life.

Unfortunately, these same setbacks also seem to explain why people give up in life: they are not prepared to make a mistake and fail. What we need to recognize as a culture is that goals are challenging and setbacks will become more frequent - you must become dependent on your ability to learn from your mistakes and overcome them.

Admitting you've made a mistake, for many reasons, is hard. We as people have an implied sense of what failure is: if you fail on a test, you're a failure, (e.g. if you make a mistake, you are a mistake, etc.).

Everything from the things we eat to someone's grades which are mostly based on test scores are not too forgiving to mistakes.

Life can be scary if you don't discover an even deeper self-identity based on courage, commitment, compassion, and creativity. You must take risks in life to become a success. Here's a few ways a person can take a risk that may involve a mistake that they can learn from:

- Do I always feel as though I am behind in my work?
- Do I want myself and my team to be more productive?
- Do I need to find a balance between work and home?
- Do my team members shirk from responsibility?
- Do I struggle with distractions?
- Do I work for a business with frequent turnaround of employees?

Four Common Ways Mistakes Are Made

Okay, let's break down the different kinds of mistakes there are. One of the first mistakes one might make would be a stupid one such as stubbing a toe, dropping a heavy object onto someone's foot, or tripping over something you may not have seen.

The next common mistake is the simple mistake - these are the kinds of mistakes people make that are avoidable but the circumstances make them inevitable. Say you're having a get-together and the power goes out because you forgot to pay your electric bill, or you're an hour late in picking up your date to the dance because you had forgotten an English essay that was due the next day at school. Those examples define what a simple mistake is.

The third most common mistake is an involved mistake - those are understood mistakes that require much effort to keep them from happening. If you arrive to work late on a frequent basis or put off something you promised you would take care of for a friend, you are making an involved mistake.

And finally, there's the complex mistake -these have complicated causes with no way to avoid them in the future such as making a tough decision that has a bad outcome or a failed relationship.

Every Outcome Has Its Own Purpose and Learning Experience

Some people enjoy making mistakes that at the time feel good in the short-term even though they have long-term consequences. Learning from simple or stupid mistakes is generally pretty easy because you'll be quick to realize what you did wrong and figure out the correct way of doing it in the future. The lessons you learn from the first two kinds of mistakes, however, are not that deep and you won't really learn anything about yourself or anyone else.

The kinds of mistakes that someone makes is what defines them as a person. There's not much to learn when you make a simple or stupid mistake.

Handling complex mistakes is slightly different in that you have to be extremely patient when you make said mistake. You should never try to fix something you do not understand because that will only make the situation worse. Try to talk to someone you can trust about what happened. They might be able to give you advice if they've been in your situation before or figure out a way to deal with the problem that you haven't yet thought of.

When you describe what happened with someone else, you can begin to break down the events that took place in chronological order and define them. Something else might have been going on that distracted you that you might realize when you're telling your story.

If more than one person is involved in a mistake, hear them out individually. They'll all emphasize aspects of the situation that stood out for them based on their circumstances which will get you a clearer picture of what really might have happened.

Getting Past Your Mistakes

Once you're able to overcome the mistake you have made, learn from it and try to focus on your life going forward. Having a sense of humor is one way of combating a person's self-esteem after they have made a mistake. When you can laugh at your mistakes, you know you've finally accepted and taken responsibility for what happened and you will no longer feel guilty or want to judge your-self because of a singular event that occurred. Humor also makes you feel better psychologically and prevents you from obsessing over something that took place in the past.

Most importantly, if you learn from your mistakes, you'll be able to avoid future mistakes. Mistakes that you make along life's road will help you achieve your goals and get you to where you want to be.

Summary

To summarize, here's what you want to do to learn from your mistakes:

- The European countries involved in WWII were heavily in debt to the US.
- The US economy was very strong and the value of dollar had appreciated.
- Of all the major world currencies, only the US dollar was backed by gold.
- The US agreed to link the dollar to the gold price of $35 per ounce and exchange gold bullion for dollars.

The Road to Wealth - Follow The Cashflow Quadrant

Financial guru Robert Kiyosaki's book "Cashflow Quadrant: Rich Dad's Guide to Financial Freedom" is a strategy guide, designed to distill and systematize the wealth of information contained in his runaway bestseller, "Rich Dad Poor Dad - What the Rich Teach Their Kids About Money - That the Poor and Middle Class Do Not!", helping readers apply those lessons to their own financial goals.

When "Rich Dad Poor Dad" was first published in 1997, it reached the top of the bestsellers lists in The New York Times, the Wall Street Journal, Business Week, USA Today and Amazon.com in a matter of days. The book has gone on to sell well over 17 million copies.

"Rich Dad Poor Dad" is a parable, describing the author's own financial education at the hands of two men: one "Poor Dad", was his own father; the other "Rich Dad" was the father of a close friend.

Three years later, Kiyosaki published "Cashflow Quadrant." Like its predecessor, the book shot to the top of bestseller lists at the New York Times, the Wall Street Journal, USA Today, and Amazon.com.

What Is The Cashflow Quadrant?

The Cashflow Quadrant is a grid illustrating the four different ways that income can be earned. The upper left quadrant is the E Quadrant: "Employee. You have a job." The bottom left quadrant is the S Quadrant: "Self Employed. You own a job." The upper right quadrant is the B Quadrant: "Business Owner. You own a system and people work for you." The bottom right quadrant is the I Quadrant: "Investor. Money works for you."

Kiyosaki believes that financial freedom is the goal every individual aspires to, and that most individuals have the potential to generate income from all four quadrants. But every individual will fall into one of these quadrants based upon his or her core beliefs and attitudes about the best way to generate income.

Kiyosaki uses the example of a physician. The physician may be on staff at a large, metropolitan hospital in which case he falls into the E Quadrant. But two days a week he may see patients out of his own office, assisted by a staff he hired and manages.

His private practice is self-employment, Quadrant S. The physician also owns a partial interest in an arterial blood gas laboratory, a business he started with three of his colleagues; these activities fall under Quadrant B. Finally, the physician invests the money he makes from the laboratory in the stock market - a Quadrant I activity.

So which of the four quadrants would best describe the physician's approach towards his finances? That would really depend upon his answer to the question, "How do you generate income?". That answer is more than just a summary of all the different ways he makes money; it's a set of distinct attitudes and personal beliefs that gets to the core of who he is as a human being.

Let's look at a few of the attitudes and beliefs embodied by each of the four quadrants.

The E Quadrant - Employee

People who fall into the E Quadrant are primarily motivated by security. They will find it difficult to understand many of the ideas of their more entrepreneurial minded cohorts in the B and I Quadrants. They depend upon their paychecks for wealth, and since their paychecks are seldom enough to buy all the things that they want, they become trapped in a cycle of buying things on credit which makes them even more dependent upon their jobs.

According to Kiyosaki, E Quadrant individuals don't understand one of the most basic laws of money: Don't try to get rich from a salary. It's not your boss's job to make you rich; it's your boss's job to make sure that you receive your paycheck on a regular basis.

The S Quadrant - Self Employed

The S Quadrant is only slightly better than the E Quadrant in achieving financial freedom. True, its members have more independence than comparable individuals in the E Quadrant, but they still have to show up for work in order to get paid. For S Quadrant individuals, money is secondary in importance to the quality of their work, which makes them highly desirable assets to B Quadrant individuals.

Self-employed S Quadrant individuals are motivated primarily by security, and secondarily by a reluctance to delegate, an almost obsessive need to do everything themselves.

They have not learned the critical importance of networking, nor the fact that time is the most important asset of all and that it is usually smarter to pay someone to do something in order to save time than it is to struggle with it yourself in order to save money.

The B Quadrant - Business Owner

B Quadrant individuals own the system that generates their income, which means they no longer have to spend time physically working. The system, if it is running smoothly, will generate income whether they are rolling up their sleeves to pitch in or not. The fact is that B Quadrant individuals most valuable contribution to the systems they've created is not routine operational work, but crafting strategy and business plans.

B Quadrant individuals are motivated by freedom and the desire to remain free by surrounding themselves with individuals and resources that can help them build their business. The B Quadrant offers an individual considerably more leverage than either the E or the S Quadrant.

The I Quadrant - Investor

The I Quadrant offers the individual the most leverage of all. This is the quadrant in which wealth is created and if one of your goals is to generate a genuinely big income, then this is the quadrant you must aspire to join, because in the I Quadrant, you're no longer working for money - money is working for you.

Not all investors are successful investors, of course. Kiyosaki divides investors into seven categories, from wannabes who spend more than they earn and individuals who go deep into debt in order to afford their investments at the bottom of the ladder to sophisticated investors and capitalists with a sound understanding of financial principles at the top.

Here is where Kiyosaki's endorsement of financial literacy kicks in. For in order to be a successful investor, you have to understand that:

- Do I always feel as though I am behind in my work?
- Do I want myself and my team to be more productive?
- Do I need to find a balance between work and home?
- Do my team members shirk from responsibility?
- Do I struggle with distractions?
- Do I work for a business with frequent turnaround of employees?

Financial Freedom

You've achieved true financial freedom when you have people working for you (B), and you have money working for you (I). Kiyosaki argues that belonging to the B Quadrant is the best prerequisite for moving into the I Quadrant, since it sharpens your judgment.

How do you move into the B Quadrant? If you're risk-adverse, forget it: you will never make the transition. Kiyosaki points out that many entrepreneurs lose two or three companies before they hit upon the business model that brings success.

The two most effective strategies for gaining B Quadrant success are joining a network marketing company, and seeking out a mentor who is accomplishing what you would like to have accomplished within the next five years.

What Are The Roots of Inspiration Deficit Disorder?

The following excerpt is taken from the book Inspiration Deficit Disorder by Jonathan H. Ellerby, Ph.D. It is published by Hay House (August 15, 2010) and available at all bookstores or online at: www.hayhouse.com.

The key difference between an inspired life (essence based) and a reactive one (Persona based) is the degree of inspiration present. Inspiration is the expression of the Essential Self and Original Source in daily life. When inspiration is a part of how you engage the world, then your attitude and experience shift to the qualities like those in the previous list.

When inspiration is missing, however, you might be successful, but you'll never be satisfied for long. Your life might look good on paper or to your friends, but you'll always feel like something is missing.

This is where Inspiration Deficit Disorder begins: with the loss of the Essential Self. It's rarely something you consciously choose; and even when you make certain sacrifices in the name of family, income, career, or society, you almost never realize that it could cost you your health, happiness, vitality, and sense of purpose or meaning. Many paths of the Persona start off seeming like a great idea, a clear road to follow. This is natural because the Persona takes its cues from outside influences and disregards the soul.

Choices in schools, hobbies, relationships, religious involvement, diet, sports, fashion, social circle, home design, and personal expression are all easily co-opted by the strong voices of peers, family, ambition, and self-promotion. Everyday advertisements and commercials prey on people's inspiration deficit. Instead of saying: "Put this magazine down and go for a walk!" or "Turn this TV off and get a life!" they say: "Buy this!", "Listen to me!" or "Act now!" . . . happiness is just a click away. If only you buy this product, you'll finally feel complete.

Dr. Wayne Dyer, a legendary author and speaker, has written about this in his own way. Recently, he also starred in the film The Shift, which explores the Persona. I like the caution he presents, highlighting that most people today feel one or all of the following three things:

- Do I always feel as though I am behind in my work?
- Do I want myself and my team to be more productive?
- Do I need to find a balance between work and home?
- Do my team members shirk from responsibility?
- Do I struggle with distractions?
- Do I work for a business with frequent turnaround of employees?

Naturally, none of these things is true. They're just passing aspects of your life, a small part of who you really are.

Five Forces of the Persona: Beware!

The last thing I want to leave you with in this chapter is a very important note about the Persona. Somehow, it takes on a momentum and life of its own.

Down the road, this will work in your favor, when you learn to align your Persona entirely with your essence. For now, this is something to be cautious of. The momentum of the Persona is rooted in five natural forces. Pay attention when they show up, as you can be pulled further and further away from your Essential Self.

The trickiest part about the forces of the Persona is that when you're unaware of the harm they can do to your health and happiness, you may actually embrace them, using them to justify why you are the way you are! These factors are intrinsic to Inspiration Deficit Disorder and will keep you stuck. As you'll see in the next chapter, the Persona gets hooked on patterns of energy and repeating cycles. It's self-perpetuating by design, so take note: it's meant to be hard to overcome.

The five forces of the Persona are:

- Do I always feel as though I am behind in my work?
- Do I want myself and my team to be more productive?
- Do I need to find a balance between work and home?
- Do my team members shirk from responsibility?
- Do I struggle with distractions?
- Do I work for a business with frequent turnaround of employees?

In my past work as a business consultant with IMPAQ (www.im-paqcorp.com), a fantastic corporation based in Los Angeles, my mentor and boss, CEO Mark Samuel, showed me how, time and time again, these five behaviors were at work in the lives of dysfunctional managers, teams, employees, and even in the culture of larger organizations. I've observed that these factors go far beyond the workplace and are universal in those who have Inspiration Deficit Disorder.

If you can work to end or minimize all or any of these, you will have begun to undo the impact of Inspiration Deficit Disorder on your life. Until you minimize, manage, or dissolve these forces, an inspiration deficit is just a step away.

1. Approval

Approval is all about the attachment to positive feedback. It isn't just about wanting to do a good job; it's about seeking recognition, wanting to be praised, affirmed, or complimented in some way. These are all forms of emotional reward and can become the motivation for a huge range of behaviors, including ones that are unhealthy and even destructive. One of the biggest problems with approval seeking is that it often looks good on the outside, but there is a disconnect on the inside.

You may be liked and appreciated, but it's exhausting. If approval doesn't follow, then you'll often feel disappointed, hurt, angered, or rejected. True soul-centered behavior needs no approval or affirmation; it is self-sufficient.

2. Judgment

Judgment is much more than just being critical. It's okay to be discerning and thoughtful, having a mind that can spot flaws. Judgment is an energy and an attitude. It holds an implied value system, that something must be bad or worse for something else to be good or best. Judgment carries a negative evaluation for anything that isn't in agreement.

It's about looking for flaws and faults with an emotional evaluation attached. Instead of saying: "This isn't my style" judgment says: "This is valueless", "This is wrong" or "That's stupid". It is oppositional and self-centered. Sadly, it feeds the Persona, and many people actually feel good when they judge others. Gossip, politics, religion, and social circles in most cultures today are overrun with judgment. Remember that it separates you from your essence.

3. Denial

Denial is one way to put off facing something. Other methods include procrastination, deliberation, avoidance, or a focus on judgment and blame. But it all adds up to denial. You are in denial when you fail to recognize or own a problem, limit, or difficult situation.

Most people don't even consciously notice or acknowledge that a problem exists. I believe that nine out of ten times the awareness is close at hand; it's just that these individuals who are in denial never take the time to allow themselves to become aware of the situation. They keep themselves distracted. This is why many people rely on blame.

4. Blame

Blame is the act of placing the responsibility for the cause or solution to a problem on another person. Usually, it's about trying to make someone else the sole source of a situation or your behavior. You may say things like: "I'd be happy if you didn't always" . . ." I'll relax when they finally stop . . . " or "I'll change when they finally admit that they. . .". Blame can be fun, and it's easy to get other people involved.

Turn on the TV and you'll see news show after news show featuring professional blamers. These expert commentators are affiliated with one view or another and blame those who are unlike them for the world's problems. Modern American popular political commentary is mostly about blaming and rarely about resolution, compromise, or problem solving.

Some people actually look good when they blame because it sounds intelligent and thoughtful. The sad part is that they remain a part of the problem instead of the solution. Be careful as you look to transform your own life. The energy of blame will show up the moment things get difficult. It usually starts with: "It's not my fault" "I have to . . ." or "I wouldn't have if only they didn't. . . ."

5. Rationalization

Rationalization means that you look for evidence to show that your fears, impulses, or habits are justified. When you rationalize, you use stories of the world and your own past to stay stuck. You might say: "Because my parents were mean to me, I don't understand kindness so I can't help being mean to you" or "I never had help. No one made it easy for me, so why should I help them?" or "I can't help being abusive because I was abused."

If you're looking for evidence to allow yourself to stay the way you are, beware! The world is so wide and full that you can find evidence for anything. Do you want to prove that something is unfair, likely to get worse, or that you have to control or react? You'll find that evidence if you look hard enough. There are lots of people making poor choices, so you can easily find someone to reference.

Don't forget that you can also find evidence for the opposite: for the best possible outcome. Be optimistic; if you look for the lesson and opportunity, you'll find it. It's a matter of perception. As the author Richard Bach once stated, if you argue for your limitations, sure enough they'll be yours.

The Five Passion Clues: How to Find Your Perfect Niche

Finding the work you feel passionate about is like solving a mystery: you have to recognize the clues that let you know you are on track. Setbacks and delays are normal; so don't get discouraged when that happens. If you try again (and again), you will discover the niche where you can reach your full potential.

Passion Clue # 1: You would do the work even if you didn't get paid for it

The first passion clue is the most difficult to grasp. Your initial reaction may be: does this mean I have to work for nothing? The answer is no and yes. No, because people gladly pay if you help, inform or entertain them. Yes, because you may need to give away what you know until you can prove you know what you are doing.

For example, are you often complimented on your ability to speak, teach, write, promote or connect with people? Do people say you are the most organized person they know, or that you won't rest until you get to the bottom of any situation? If so isn't it time you got paid for what you do so naturally and well?

Passion clue # 2: Mastery is your goal

The desire for mastery is the basis of success in work and life. You are not wishing you were somewhere else, wondering if you are missing out on the latest trend, or worrying that competitors are outdoing you. Nor do you take shortcuts when you get frustrated.

Look at the past and you will see that you succeeded when you were self-disciplined. When things got hard you thought about giving up but you kept going in spite of your fears. When others said you didn't have what it took to succeed, you turned a deaf ear.

After you crossed the finish line you had what no one could take away from you, the knowledge that you did what was difficult for you, in spite of the risks.

Passion Clue #3: You are transformed as you do the work

Transformation means that you are not the person you were when you started your work is not who you are now. As the years go by, you keep learning and growing and increasing your value in the marketplace, expertise that makes you virtually recession-proof.

Becoming who you were designed to be is life's greatest achievement. Change for the better can be scary, since letting go of the past stirs up primal fear: What if I'm wrong? What if I fail? Why can't I just stay where I am?

Passion is a ruthless friend: it will not let you settle for the easy glide through life. And so you move forward, trusting the new you will be much better than the old.

Passion Clue #4: You are not aware that time is passing by

A sense of timelessness is another clue you are on the passion path. You wake up in the morning and the next thing you know it is evening. But as soon as fear enters your mind boundaries go up and you are in the past or the future, worrying about what you can't control. If you can turn off the mental horror movie for a moment your mind quiets down, as when you wake up from a nightmare. Then you realize fear determines your experience of time. The less fear, the more you are where there is no time.

Don't confuse a sense of timelessness with vagueness, being late, forgetting appointments and responsibilities. Drifting along in a dreamy fog is not living in the moment; it is passive avoidance. Like a house that is always free of clutter, you don't worry about details when you live in the moment; you just take care of them. You are right here, right now, ready to seize opportunity by the forelock.

Passion Clue # 5: You are paid to be who you are

When you were growing up you were taught that you were your family, nationality, religion, race and gender. Later, you were defined by what peers and authority figures thought of you. As an adult, your value is measured by your education and training, your accomplishments, possessions, the money you make, friends, who you live with or marry, your children, grandchildren and what they achieve. But who are you without anything and anyone to define you?

If you were in a strange country where you knew no one and no one knew you, who are you then? When you get paid to be this person, your authentic self, you are definitely on the passion path.

It may take several tries before you discover the niche that is just right for you, the place where you will reach your full potential and make the money you need. Like Goldilocks, you have to test all the beds before you find the one that suits the real you. Then (surprise!) you discover that getting there was all the fun.

About the author:

Nancy Anderson is a nationally acclaimed career consultant based in the San Francisco Bay Area. Now in private practice, she previously worked for two prestigious career consulting firms. Nancy has also hosted her own radio program on KGO in San Francisco. She is the author of the bestselling career guide, Work with Passion: How to Do What You Love for a Living. She lives in Northern California and her website is www.workwithpassion.com.

Based on the book Work with Passion in Midlife and Beyond. Copyright © 2010 by Nancy Anderson. Reprinted with permission of New World Library, Novato, CA. www.newworldlibrary.com or 800/972-6657 ext. 52.

The Instant Millionaire:
A Tale of Wisdom and Wealth

Why do some people succeed in becoming millionaires while others only dream about it? What do they know that others don't?

The answer to these questions is at the heart of of The Instant Millionaire: A Tale of Wisdom and Wealth (New World Library, August 2010). Written by millionaire Mark Fisher, this memorable fable is based on the true story of his meeting with an old man who passed on the secrets of his success.

In this excerpt, from chapter one we meet the book's main character, a young man who is fed up at with a nightmare job and dreaming of something more.

Let The Story Begin...

There was once a bright young man who wanted to get rich. He had had his fair share of disappointments and setbacks, it couldn't be denied, and yet he still believed in his lucky star.

While he waited for fortune to smile, he worked as an assistant to an account executive in a small advertising agency. He was inadequately paid and had felt for some time that his job offered him little satisfaction. His heart was simply no longer in it.

He dreamed of doing something else, perhaps writing a novel that would make him wealthy and famous and end his financial problems once and for all. But wasn't his ambition a bit unrealistic? Did he really have enough talent and technique to write a bestseller, or would the pages be filled with the bleak, unfocused ramblings of his inner misery?

His job had been a daily nightmare for more than a year. His boss spent most of each morning reading the newspaper and writing memos before disappearing to indulge in a three-hour lunch. He also changed his mind continually and gave contradictory orders.

But it wasn't only his boss, he was surrounded by colleagues who were also fed up with what they were doing. They seemed to have abandoned any sense of vision; they seemed to have given up altogether. He didn't dare tell any of them about his fantasy of dropping everything and becoming a writer. He knew they would treat it as a joke. When he was at work he often felt cut off from the world, as if he was in a foreign country, unable to speak the language.

Every Monday morning he wondered how on earth he was going to survive another week at the office. He felt totally alienated from the files piled high on his desk, from the needs of clients clamoring to sell their cigarettes, their cars, their beer....

He had written a letter of resignation six months earlier and had walked into his boss's office a dozen times with the letter burning in his pocket, but he had never been quite able to go through with it. It was funny; he would not have hesitated three or four years ago, but now he seemed unsure of what to do. Something was holding him back, some kind of force, or was it simply cowardice? He seemed to have lost the nerve that had always helped him get what he wanted in the past.

He kept waiting till the time was ripe, finding all kinds of excuses for not jumping into action, wondering if he could ever really succeed. Has he turned into a perpetual dreamer?

Did his paralysis spring from the fact that he was saddled with debts? Or was it because he had simply started to get old, a process inevitably triggered the minute we give up our visions of the future?

One day, when he was feeling especially frustrated, he suddenly thought of visiting an uncle of his who had become a millionaire. Perhaps he might be able to give him some advice, or better yet, some money.

His uncle was a warm, friendly person who immediately agreed to see him. He refused to lend him any money, however, claiming he wouldn't be doing him a favor.

"How old are you?" his uncle asked, after listening to his tale of woe.

"Thirty-two" the young man whispered timidly.

"Do you know that by the time J. Paul Getty was twenty-three he already made his first million? And that when I was your age, I had half a million? So how in the world is it that you are forced to borrow money at your age?"

"Beats me. I work like a dog, sometimes over fifty hours a week...."

"Do you really believe that hard work is what makes people rich?"

"I...I guess so...anyway, that's what I've always been led to believe."

"How much do you make a year $35,000?"

"Yeah, about that much replied the young man."

"Do you think that someone who earns $350,000 works ten times as many hours a week as you do? Obviously not! So if this person earns ten times more than you do without working any more than you do, then he must be doing something quite differently than you. He must have a secret you are totally unaware of."

"That must be true."

"You're lucky you understand that at least. Most people don't even get that far. They're far too busy trying to earn a living to stop and think about how they could get rid of their money problems. Most people don't even spend an hour of their time trying to figure out how they could get rich and why they've never managed to do so."

The young man had to admit that, despite his burning ambition and his dream of making a fortune, he had never taken the time to really think his situation through. Everything seemed to distract him and prevent him from facing up to a task that was obviously of fundamental importance.

The young man's uncle was silent for a while, then smiled.

"I've decided to help you out. I'm going to send you to the man who helped me get rich. He's called the Instant Millionaire. Have you heard of him?"

"No, never" the young man said.

"He chose that name because he claims he became a millionaire overnight after discovering the true secret of making a fortune.

He claims he can help anyone become a millionaire overnight, or at least acquire the mentality of a millionaire."

His uncle turned to a large map on the wall and pointed to a small, somewhat isolated town.

"Have you ever been there?"

"No."

"Why not give it a try? Go and find him. He just might reveal his secret to you. He lives in a fantastic house, the most beautiful one in the whole town. You shouldn't have any problem finding it."

"Why don't you just tell me the secret? Then I won't have to take the trouble of going there."

"Simply because I don't have the right to. When the Instant Millionaire confided it to me, the first thing he did was make me swear never to tell it to anybody. However, he did say I could refer people to him."

All of this seemed both surprising and involved to the young man. It certainly aroused his curiosity.

"Are you sure you can't tell me anything? Anything at all?"

"Absolutely positive. What I can do is recommend you highly to the Instant Millionaire."

The young man's uncle pulled out a sheet of elegant writing paper from a drawer in his massive oak desk, took his pen, and hastily scribbled a few lines. He then folded the letter, put it in an envelope, and handed it to his nephew.

"Here's your introduction" he said, and here's the millionaire's address. One last thing. You must promise not to read this letter. If ever you do open it, despite my warning, and you still want it to work for you, you'll have to pretend that you haven't opened it. But how can you undo what's already been done?"

The young man didn't have the vaguest idea what his uncle was talking about, but he agreed. His uncle had always been a bit eccentric, and he was doing him a favor, after all, so he decided not to press the point. He thanked him warmly and left.

How to Reach The Summit of Your Everest

The following excerpt is taken from the book The Everest Principle: How to Achieve the Summit of Your Life by Stephen Brewer, M.D. and Peggy Wagner, L.P.C. It is published by Hay House (February 2010) and is available at all bookstores or online at www.hayhouse.com.

If you want to be happy, set a goal that commands your thoughts, liberates your energy, and inspires your hopes. - Andrew Carnegie

It stands alone as a challenge and a dare. With its jagged snow-capped peaks, the highest mountain on this earth is 29,035 feet above sea level. Men and women, experts and novices, have always been both intimidated and intoxicated by, and unexplainable drawn to, this natural wonder, which is located on the border between Nepal and Tibet. Ancient tribes called it Sagarmatha, but the world now knows it by two words that loom larger than life: Mount Everest.

Those who climb the mountain summit range in age, the youngest climber in history being a 16-year-old Sherpa who was told she was much too young, but something inside drove her up those peaks (an 18-year-old California woman was the youngest climber from the West).

Men and women in their 40s and 50s have been informed by doctors and hysterical loved ones that they were much too old to climb the mountain. Something in their nature drove them to grab their oxygen bottles, pull on those hiking boots, invest in some ropes, and begin climbing sometimes not even knowing why it was so life affirming to them to scale those rock walls. They simply had to do it.

As with any life challenge, there are risks. For example, the eight men and women who perished in 1996 during a storm high on the mountain became the basis for a best-selling book, appropriately titled Into Thin Air. The others who have perished didn't do so in vain, but remain heroes and examples of cautionary tales.

Climbers have often been faced with horrifying and spirit-crushing setbacks in their quest, including treacherous winds, violent monsoons, breath-stealing heat, and beautiful snowstorms that later turned into eardrum-numbing avalanches. But the climbers arrive day after day from every country in the world. They have different political and religious backgrounds, but looking up at those razor-sharp peaks, they are exactly the same, with one goal: to reach the sky.

They push on because Mount Everest is just like life: quitting is not allowed.

As in life, the climbers make use of helpful tools and friendly cohorts, which in this case include yaks, human porters, ropes, ladders, and the few supplies they can carry with them in their packs. Their journey is often met with the unexpected, but that's also like life. One day you can walk across what looks like a very slippery patch of ice and by some grace you remain upright and unscathed. Your confidence is bolstered, and you tackle the next tough patch.

Then there are other days when you don't even see the ice; you take one step and then comes the hard fall.

Why bother with any of the above? The climbers know what we will teach you in this book. Scaling your own personal Mount Everest is worth it for many reasons, including the idea that the journey is often more rewarding than the destination.

That's not to say we don't believe in reaching one's own personal summit. Just like on Everest, those who hit their own heights are figuratively on top of the world.

Welcome to The Everest Principle

This book was written because we're guessing you're not about to take a quick trip to the real Mount Everest and call a local Sherpa for some climbing advice. In fact, this book has very little to do with the skill and art of mountain climbing, although we believe it's an amazing sport and bow our heads to those who take on those sheer rock walls.

Mount Everest will serve as the metaphor in the journey of these pages, because we believe that all of us have our own personal Everest to scale each and every day. As the tallest mountain on the planet, Everest will represent the highest goal that we can set for ourselves at any one time whether that means creating a new life, launching a business, overcoming illness, securing a desired promotion, training for a marathon, or losing weight.

Reaching the summit of your Everest, whatever goal it may be attached to, requires planning and effort on your part. Those climbers on Everest don't just go out there in a tank top and a pair of shorts and hit base camp, asking: "Do we need anything to get up there?"

A successful climber doesn't simply wake up one morning and start walking up a tall mountain guided by inspiration alone. Attaining a lofty goal demands mental preparation and physical stamina, fueled by some important tools, including proper nutrition and good health.

We chose Everest as our mental guide throughout this book because those who reach the summit are at the top of their game. They're showing us what's often called peak performance. That's a term that has frequently been used in association with elite athletes or even fast cars, which means demonstrating an ability to fulfill one's potential despite any odds against it.

But peak performance, similar to what climbers on Everest exhibit, is something we can tailor to our lives no matter what path we're on or what goals occupy our dreams at night. The tools we need to start with in this case aren't sturdy hiking boots or a bottle of oxygen, although we might get a little breathless at times . . . in a good way. What's required is simply the motivation to be the best that you can be.

Most of us know how easy it is to drift into boredom and lethargy, or even hopelessness and despair, when life doesn't work in the way we've planned. In recent times, with the economy sinking, homes landing in foreclosure, and personal wealth disappearing, we've seen many people fall into the traps of fear and depression. They wonder if they even have the juice to push on to make their ever-fading dreams come true.

We believe that there has never been a better time to challenge yourself with high but realistic and attainable goals. You don't need to settle for mediocrity in your life or live in fear.

You don't have to lower your expectations about what you're capable of achieving, despite any setbacks. You shouldn't allow your past failures to cloud your perceptions of future success.

No matter what stage of life you find yourself in whether you've entered retirement or just graduated from college there's an Everest left to climb that will add renewed purpose and meaning to your life. You can take yourself to this higher level of goal setting and performance without sacrificing

other important aspects of your way of being. That's because true peak performance is about maintaining balance and bringing other people along with you as you make the climb up your own personal mountain.

About the authors:

Stephen C. Brewer, M.D., is the Medical Director of the world-renowned Canyon Ranch Health Resort in Tucson, Arizona. He is a board-certified family physician with a subspecialty in integrative medicine. Dr. Brewer and his co-author, Peggy Wagner, have developed a Peak Performance program whose purpose is to help individuals excel in their health and their goals, both personally and professionally.

Peggy Wagner is a Licensed Professional Counselor (LPC) at Canyon Ranch Health Resort in Tucson, Arizona. A graduate of the University of Vermont, she has been trained in hypnosis, EMDR, and other life-enhancement techniques. Peggy also speaks nationally and internationally on peak performance and other wellness topics. Her work has been featured in prisons, Native American reservations, alternative schools, hospitals, and drug-and-alcohol treatment centers.

Five Financial Keys
That Go Against Traditional Wisdom

In his latest best-seller, "Rich Dad's Increase Your Financial IQ" Robert Kiyosaki takes his tried-and-true financial strategies to the next level.

Kiyosaki's driving principle in the book is for readers to understand that to make money, you must first develop the financial intelligence that can continually and residually, make money.

With a strong understanding of what it means to develop your "Financial IQ" Kiyosaki provides five points that not only go against conventional wisdom, but will ensure an exponential increase of your wealth.

The Five Financial IQs

1. How to Increase Your Money

According to Kiyosaki, the key to making money is to solve problems. Most people today seek the latest and greatest gimmick that will make them rich, quick. But, will they stay rich? Probably not. They do not know how to maintain their income or how to make their money work for them.

Solving problems may seem like general advice, but Kiyosaki further explains that the real question to ask yourself is, which problems you want to solve. What are you naturally good at? If you are a good salesman, then sell. If you are an artist, then create more masterpieces. Make a profit. Use what you have.

However, perhaps the best advice from this chapter is to remember that solving problems is a process.Do not let fear hold you back. Continue on. Persevere. Becoming rich is not an event, it is a process that you need to continue to build.

2. How to Protect Your Money

With Financial IQ as your weapon, Kiyosaki urges the financially driven to protect your money. A lesson he learned in the 80's when he lost everything, declared bankruptcy, paid creditors, and fought back, Kiyosaki wants you to know that you can do better today than you did back then.

He recommends circumventing seven financial predators to protect your money:

A. Bureaucrats While Kiyosaki recognizes the importance of paying taxes, he indicates that the majority of people do not understand how to legally pay the lower end of taxes. He divides the US tax system into three categories:

- Do I always feel as though I am behind in my work?
- Do I want myself and my team to be more productive?
- Do I need to find a balance between work and home?
- Do my team members shirk from responsibility?
- Do I struggle with distractions?

- Do I work for a business with frequent turnaround of employees?

B. Bankers Contrary to how some might feel, the banks may not be your friend. Hiding in the form of fees and changing interest rates, it is important to keep your money moving. Kiyosaki also elucidates the myth of the U.S. Federal Reserve Bank.He states that the phrase is very misleading in that the U.S. Federal Reserve Bank is NOT:

- The European countries involved in WWII were heavily in debt to the US.
- The US economy was very strong and the value of dollar had appreciated.
- Of all the major world currencies, only the US dollar was backed by gold.
- The US agreed to link the dollar to the gold price of $35 per ounce and exchange gold bullion for dollars.

C. Brokers Dealing with brokers will only make you broke. They know how to work the system and make the profit. They may not have your best intentions at heart. Instead, Kiyosaki suggests seeking those brokers who are students of their profession and actually invest in what they sell.

D. Businesses Using wisdom in what you purchase and where will benefit you in the long run. He drives home the fact that not everything will make you rich. Determine what it is that can. Steer clear of having a "poor person" mentality where buying products at a high interest rate will make you the fool and paying for it for years beyond what it is worth.

E. Brides and Beaus All looking to enter a marriage should invest in a prenuptial agreement to protect your finances.

F. Brothers-in-law Generally, here, Kiyosaki illustrates the importance of executing a will and trust to protect your financial worth from those seeking to prey on your assets rather than those who you wish to inherit it actually receive it.

G. Barristers Defined as those who legally take money from you through court and legal fees, Kiyosaki proposes holding assets in the names of legal entities as opposed to your own name and buying insurance before needed rather than when the event arises.

Think of the money in your pocket. Now think of your pocket lined with holes. Protecting your money is to first locate the hole, then find ways to stop them from further leaking.

3. How to Budget Your Money

When times get tough, Kiyosaki notes that most people immediately begin cutting back on their expenses. However, as much as this may help, Kiyosaki reasons that sometimes this may be unnecessary when you prioritize your spending and create the money you plan to save as a fixed number, enable your assets to pay for your liabilities in the long run, and know when to spend and when to cut back.

4. Leveraging Your Money

Money is not about how much you have but about how you use it. The widespread belief that debt is bad is actually wrong. It is great to have good debt, such as a house as leverage. Bad debt, such as credit cards, will make you poor fast. Leveraging your time along with your money will take you even further. Kiyosaki stresses, It,s not what you make; it's what you keep.

5. Improving Your Financial Information

Kiyosaki counsels the wise to understand that gold is not going up and hasn't since 1971 when President Nixon took America off the gold standard and made the US dollar the reserve currency of the world. He underlines this event as why the US dollar has lost 80% of its purchasing power and the price of gas, food, and homes, has skyrocketed.

Furthermore, don't save your money. Rather, place a hedge of protection around it by betting against the US dollar rather than guessing an industry. The prediction is that every time money is made into a currency, the value becomes zero.

Tips to Survive Financially in the Wake of the Recession

The last several years have witnessed the greatest economic collapse for the United States since the Great Depression of the 1930's. This quadruple tidal wave perfect storm encompassed a housing collapse, banking crises, credit crunch, and unemployment rout all at once.

The end result that you have been left with is housing prices that are down thirty-five percent; hundreds of failed banks and financial corporations, including the largest savings and loan Washington Mutual, historic and legendary investment house Lehman Brothers, and former world's largest insurance company AIG; and an unemployment rate that hovers stubbornly between nine and a half and ten percent.

It is no wonder that experts given to lyricism have termed this economic crisis the Great Recession. Despite all of the fanfare that accompanied the new administration into the White House, things have barely improved for the national economy, if they have really improved at all, in the first year plus since the new team took office.

All of this has affected you, the real American on the ground, in frustrating and sometimes terrible ways.

Even if you have managed to hold on to a secure job, you are likely struggling with a reduced access to credit, a significantly depreciated house value, and a substantially diminished in value retirement and investment portfolio.

The bad news is that no one can say for sure what the economic cards will look like in the near and medium term future. The good news is that you can survive, and maybe even get ahead, financially in the swamping wake of the Great Recession, if you only take to heart a number of the following actionable tips.

Read About Surviving the Great Recession

Reading this article is a good first step. There are a number of excellent books that have been published about recessions in general and in particular the one that the country is struggling to crawl out of now.

You should either buy, or better still borrow, the book Financial Reckoning Day: Surviving the Soft Depression of the Twenty-First Century, by William Bonner, as well as a copy of Aftershock: Protect Yourself and Profit in the Next Global Financial Meltdown by Robert Wiedemer, David Wiedemer, and Cindy Spitzer.

Both of these books give practical and detailed advice on how to position yourself to not only tread water when your friends and neighbors are sinking, but also to swim to land. This makes you feel like less of a victim, and more like you are in control of your own fate.

Think About Changing Fields to a Critical Sector

It is true that not everyone will be in the position to do this in the wake of the Great Recession. Still, recessions tend to be times when you can go back to school to re-position yourself in a more secure job field for the future.

Should you consider this, you will want to think along the lines of health care, government jobs, or food producing and supplying careers. In good times and bad, you will find that these jobs survive the turmoil. While you are retooling, be sure to avoid construction types of jobs or management jobs in retail businesses. These are the most likely to be eliminated in a restrictive and tightening economic scenario.

Start Up a Small Home Based Business

Although this may sound counter intuitive to you, the best time to begin a new low overhead venture out of your house is when times are hard and things are tight. This is when your motivation to create extra ways to make money is at its highest.

Starting a small home based business does not need to be difficult either. Focus on something that you are interested in or have some ability in, such as taking pictures, writing articles, making crafts, or tutoring. All of these business can be done in whole or part over the Internet these days. For those who love photography, stock photo websites are widespread now, and they are paying people for collections of pictures for their clients.

An example of these are the completely free websites Fotolia, Shutterstock, Featurepics, and Dreamstime.

Those who enjoy and have some skill at writing can become a free-lance writer for sites ranging from eHow.com to eLance.com, to textbroker.com. All of these sites pay writers for articles and other writing related assignments, and they are all free to join. Those who are crafty can make handicrafts and sell them on eBay.com.

Finally, for those who like to tutor students and have some ability with it, there is Tutor.com, the world's largest online tutoring outfit. Other advantages that you will find in working at home include reduced fuel expenditures and child care costs. Whatever small home based business that you start up, it is likely to provide at the least some extra income that will help you get through the wake of the Great Recession.

Avoid New Debts and Save Money

If there is one lesson that the Great Recession has reminded you, it should be that your capability of surviving in hard times is is lessened by any debt, and not just excessive debt. It is a good idea for you to learn to make do with less money than you make. In this way, you will find that you are able to save up a great deal more money that you did in the past. Economists have been telling you for years that you should have six months worth of your income saved up for hard times. Having seen how the Great Recession ravaged so many people and families, now you know why.

Reduce Outlays By Changing Service Providers

The idea behind this suggestion is not that you should stop using your utilities, cable, Internet, or cell phone, as that would not be either practical or much fun.

Instead, look into competing services that might offer you a better deal than your current cell phone provider, cable television provider, Internet provider, gas provider, insurance company, and even bank are willing to offer you. You will be astonished at how much money you can save by doing something as simple as bundling your phone, cable, Internet, and sometimes cell phone services into a single provider.

Downsize Your Current or Next Vehicle

Many of you are still driving those gas guzzling megalith Sport Utility Vehicles that resemble a train more than they do a car. You might sell the monster, or trade it in, in favor of a smaller, more economical vehicle that offers you better gas mileage. Every time you visit the gas station, you will feel a little bit better about living in the wake of the Great Recession this way.

Take Advantage of the Situation to Profit

A final proactive thing that you might do in a recession like the Great Recession is to look at the prices of depreciated assets around you. If you do have some money that you saved from the plummeting stock market a few years ago, then you will find that the prices on stocks and other assets like battered down Real Estate present a truly tremendous buying opportunity.

The key lies in finding the best such assets that you can, and then buying them with the intention of holding on to them for several years, or even for five years. The profits that you can make in this way will help you to survive not only the wake of the present Great Recession, but any others that may come your way in the future.

Every recession is nothing else than a wealth transfer. Educate yourself financially and find out where the wealth is transferred.

The Wealth Mindset Conquers All Money Myths

Let's start out with what wealth is. Wealth is the abundance of valuable resources or material possessions (assets), or the control of such assets. An individual, community, region or country that possesses an abundance of such possessions or resources is known as wealthy.

The word 'wealth' is related to ideas of health and well-being: to be 'wealthy' is to experience abundant good health and well-being.

Money Myth #1: The US Dollar has Intrinsic Value

Most people think that wealth and money are the same thing, and so they mostly aim for money, which is a huge mistake in terms of an overall strategy of wealth. Seeking lots of money per se does not usually lead to true wealth.

When you go into the bank with your dollar you can only exchange it for another dollar. Like other market-driven systems, supply and demand have some influence on the value of the dollar beyond its denomination. More dollars in circulation mean a lesser value; less dollars in circulation mean a higher value.

Without any increase in productivity every dollar falls more when more dollars are pushed into circulation. This has been the standard case since 1971, with the dollar losing more real purchasing power each year up to present.

"A nickel ain't worth a dime anymore."

- Yogi Berra

Since 1971 - when Nixon took the US dollar off the gold standard - money in the United States and in many other nations that followed suit, became fiat money or simple currency. Fiat currencies like the present US dollar are not backed up by real assets of any kind, including gold. As a fiat currency, the US dollar's value is only what the US Treasury Department and the Federal Reserve say it is, an imaginary value that has no ultimate relationship to the true asset wealth of the country.

Seeking more fiat money or currency is a dead end. It is as illogical to reason that because it is six o'clock in the morning, the sun will rise. Sunrises are not intrinsic to mechanical timekeeping. The fact is, the sun rises regardless of abstractions like clocks or other human conveniences. Currency is one such human convenience for governments that has no intrinsic value - other than the slight value of paper and ink it takes to print it.

On the other hand, wealth does has intrinsic value, and can have noticeable effects within the economy by producing something or providing a service to others. Goods and services each are assigned some value, which then can be transferred into other goods and services via currency.

Money Myth #2: Chasing After Money is Better than Being in Business

Wealth, the transfer of goods and services, therefor increases the economic status of a monetary system or a market over time, which results in an increase in the standard of living. Merely chasing after, hoarding or manipulating a particular currency diminishes the overall value of the economy. No goods are produced. No services are produced.

That's the simple reason why wealthy businesses and investors get taxed less than employed people. They simply provide more economic value, no real intrinsic value, in a system that places a high premium on simply moving money around rather than on the more labor intensive goods and services it takes to make society function in the real world. It can feel unfair for hard working people everywhere, but that's the truth behind the discrepancies built into our tax structure and economic system.

Your task becomes this: Use this knowledge to your advantage.

Currency chasers usually only care for themselves and believe that they need to get as much as they can to make a living or to survive. It can be quite a high adrenalin game to chase after ever increasing amounts of funny money. People that accumulate wealth, on the other hand, are mostly business people, which produce goods or provide some kind of service.

Money flows from the production of these goods and services, value is added to the economy, and personal and business wealth accumulates provided production is met, services are in demand and margins are controlled. It is easy to understand that business persons have a much different motivation than currency chasers. It is also easy to see that the outcome in each case is usually quite different over time as well.

Business promotes stability. Currency chasing promotes excitement. Which would you feel more comfortable placing your faith in? Stability or excitement?

A person with a wealth mindset will never be broke although he or she may run out of money temporally. Because those with this mindset are interested in serving others, they think differently. They put themselves on the line every time they offer a good or service, and try to always put the customer or client first. Money comes as a result of their wealth mindset.

Money Myth #3: Lots of Money Equals Lots of Happiness Forever

There are endless stories and statistics of people that won the lottery or received a large sum of money through an inheritance. In 95% of all cases the money was gone within a year and they found themselves exactly where they were before.

They did not have the necessary mindset to build value into their windfalls. They didn't create anything in terms of products or service. Rather, they fell into the trap of pandering to that pervasive social disease of our time: rampant consumerism. They spent themselves out of a chance at a new life.

Now you understand why a wealth mindset is the starting point to become wealthy. Without a wealthy mindset and the fundamental understanding of its principles you will never become truly wealthy.

That's why I have created an affirmation audio session for you. In this audio session you will listen to 25 wealth affirmations. An affirmation is basically nothing more nor less than a declaration that something is true.

The Law of Attraction and many other current books use affirmations as a way of pointing out that your thoughts and believes create the reality you perceive.

This wealth audio session is about 18 minutes long and short enough to listen to at least once every day, which I highly recommend. You can do this when you have free time or before you go to sleep. Do not use it when you are active in any way, e.g. while driving your car.

This audio session contains binaural beats and isochronic tones that help you to relax and also support your brain to be more receptive to these new wealth suggestions. There are no subliminal (hidden) messages, all affirmations are clear and clearly spoken out loud.

If you want to do bonus work, then repeat in your mind each affirmation after you hear it.

This session is available for members only. If you are not a member yet, you can sign up here for free. Also included in your membership is a 30 minutes personal financial coaching session with one of our team members. This offer is time limited - so check it out now.

The One Habit That Will Lead You to Financial Freedom

The majority of people around the world are struggling to squeeze out enough money to support their mere existence day in and day out.

You may have heard it said that around five percent of the people today either partially control or outright own in excess of ninety-five percent of the resources.

There are countries where the numbers prove to be worse than this, too. Despite the shocking fact that as few as five out of every one hundred people that you pass on the street control most of the wealth, the truth is that this is no accident.

Attitude and action makes all of the difference between the rich and the poor in the present day United States.

Attitude Differences Between the Rich and the Poor

There are many explanations given to you for why the rich have almost all of the money and the poor have practically none of it. Perhaps you have heard the following story told to illustrate a point. If all of the money in the entire world were taken away from the wealthy, and then distributed equally to all people, then everyone would have the same amount of money for a drastic change.

In less than twenty years time, those who were formerly wealthy would have all of the money back again. How can it be true that only twenty years would be required for all of the money to migrate out of the hands of the poor back into the pockets of the rich?

Attitude is what makes most of the difference between the rich and the poor in this world. To put it simply, the wealthy prove to be those individuals who understand the importance of having a positive attitude towards the law of attraction. These persons who have money are never content with settling for only a little of something when they can instead utilize the thing to gain more substance in their lives.

Another way of saying this is that the have's believe in their hearts that they possess a right to be wealthy. Their thoughts and actions dwell on riches and money. Those millionaires and billionaires know that abundance is out there for the taking, if only one is willing to put forth the effort to make it happen.

In contrast, the poor grasp hold of a mindset that tells them that they can not have money, success, and happiness. They believe that the system is set up to their disadvantage. Beyond this, they are convinced that they will never attain wealth. These thoughts and convictions translate into their actions.

This means that they then act as though they can never become wealthy. It should come as no surprise to you that as a result of this thought process that leads to inaction, they in fact never get rich. Most any person with the proper attitude that leads to the right actions can become rich; this is an important concept that you may have heard, and one that escapes from the mentality of the poor entirely.

The Rich Make Their Own World

A marked difference that you will find distinguishing the poor and middle classes from the rich is that the rich aggressively create their own scenarios and even world. The wealthy are not content in simply accepting the circumstances in which they find themselves. Instead, they set about proactively changing it.

The middle classes and the poor hold on to their epileptic mentality instead. It tells them that given enough time, things will simply change by themselves. Perhaps if they play the lottery long or often enough, then it will be their turn to win the millions in the jackpot. They are either not aware or have forgotten completely that time all alone will not improve or alter the situation. Only a person can do this. When people are constantly giving up their responsibilities to other people or even the Federal government, then they are not taking the proper action to change their world.

A great example of this proactive mindset lies in the different attitudes towards saving and the importance of saving that people in the two extreme categories hold. *The rich make it a habit and practice to pay themselves first when their salaries come in.*

They understand that by waiting until after the bills and expenses are all covered that probably little to nothing will be left over. You have probably experienced personally the consistent truth that bills and expenses have a nasty habit of expanding to take up all of the available money. The poor instead struggle to first pay their bills. If they find any money left when this is done, which is not often, then they think about saving some money.

The Rich Are Never Satisfied

Even though the wealthy are already rich and have plenty of money and assets, they do not use this as an excuse to take it easy for the remainder of their lives. Instead, they continue to put forth efforts to increase their money still more. They do this by developing wealth building systems and putting them to work constantly.

They also know that saving is not as sensible as is investing money. Rather than only struggle to save money, like the middle classes and the poor do, they instead invest it in stocks, real estate, investment properties or another source that can generate income. The rich are never satisfied with the money that they possess, and this motivates them to keep trying to generate and gather more money.

The Rich Spend a Smaller Amount of Money and They Spend it from Their Gains

A sense of thrift is necessary to achieve wealth. You may like or hate this idea, but it remains the biggest mental hurdle for the middle classes and poor to overcome. More should be saved and invested, and less spent, at every time when it proves to be possible. Not only this, but the poor spend the money they earn in their paychecks. The rich, on the other hand, are only spending money out of that which they generate as income from assets.

The Rich Spend Less and Invest More

You have heard this again and again. You must spend less money and invest more of it instead. Attaining financial freedom comes from the understanding of how to multiply the money that you hold within your hand. Money has the somewhat unique properties about it that it reproduces itself when used and invested wisely.

This means that every dollar that you hold has the power to move you to either greater wealth or greater poverty. It will be for greater wealth if you put the money wisely to work for you. It will be towards greater poverty if you fritter it away instead. The choice is yours. Either demonstrate a positive attitude, and resulting proactive actions, that lead towards wealth, or have instead the negative attitude, and accompanying lack of effective actions, that keep one poor and from achieving his or her dreams.

Make it your most important habit to pay yourself first each month.

The Secret To Personal Wealth Is Financial Education

Since the investor, businessman, and self help guru Robert Kiyosaki burst onto the personal financial market, he has written an impressive fifteen books that have a total combined in excess of twenty-six million copies sold.

You probably know of him as the owner and creator of the Rich Dad, Poor Dad concept brand. Robert has put out several books in this series. One of these is "Conspiracy of the Rich," which is reviewed in the following paragraphs.

Robert's Unique Take on Personal Finance

You will find that Robert Kiyosaki is beloved by many readers as a result of his one of a kind take on personal finance and economics in general. Unlike many financial gurus, he does not accept at face value anything put out by the government, financial managers, or the financial media unless he is able to prove it himself, through his own research efforts. So that you know, he does not claim to be the most intelligent man on the planet. You can not deny that he has successfully learned how to earn a great amount of money, especially through developing, promoting, and then selling his original ideas.

Ideas of "Conspiracy of the Rich"

Robert's newer book is "Conspiracy of the Rich." It contains a great deal of helpful and sound information while proving to be an easy read. You will see that the main idea that he wishes to impart is that we are in the midst of an ongoing economic collapse. He offers a good amount of advice about how to survive and thrive in it.

Your Wait for Systemic Change is Futile

When you read the book, you will probably come across a few ideas with which you may personally disagree. For example, Robert would prefer not to attempt to alter our political system, even though he believes it is the core of the problem. Without significant changes, he points out, you and all Americans will suffer financially. On top of this, he claims that the majority of the middle class will be totally ruined.

Robert says that a great number of Americans like yourself are simply waiting around for the world's financial and political systems to change. In his opinion, that is simply wasting time. He believes that it is simpler to change himself and yourself than it is to wait around for both your leaders, as well as the system, to change.

Your Personal Wealth is in Danger

Kiyosaki builds on this concept to convince you that you have the power to gain control over your financial future. The fact that you are probably a member of the middle class that will be eliminated does not daunt him. He suggests that the shadowy individuals controlling the financial world do not want you to know what is really going on.

Robert is comfortable with these scary claims because he believes that he and some of his readers like you will manage to avoid the coming crash.

Maybe both Robert and you his reader will avoid the collapse, but one thing that he does not sufficiently address is how you will manage to shelter your salvaged wealth from an increasingly tyrannical government. Surely as a desperate American government moves closer to the hyperinflation that he suggests is coming soon, they will be looking for any money making ventures to aggressively tax that they can find.

A Government Conspiracy

Robert spends the next significant section of the book talking about the four primary reasons for why your wealth is slipping through your fingers today. These are taxes, inflation, debt, and standard retirement planning via 401k's. He paints you a scenario of how the super rich use both the Treasury and the Federal Reserve in order to gain control over all of the world in their appetite for wealth and power.

Kiyosaki says that the wealthy are always tempted to hold back part of their workers' fair wages and to be dishonest in their trade contracts and dealings so that they might grow both their money and influence. They are furthermore tempted to utilize their riches in order to create political power. They use this to make laws which serve to safeguard their companies from competitors and also provide them with significant competitive advantages.

While this is all going on, the poor feel tempted to desire the riches of the wealthy. This in turn leads the poor to organized complaining that gets the poor together to vote as a block and elect leaders who redistribute the wealth. They take it from the wealthy and hard working individuals and give it out to the poor instead. In such a way, Robert says, the middle class and poor work in concert to utilize the American political system in order to rob their neighbors.

Kiyosaki claims that both groups are at the root of the present and coming financial collapse. What the poor should be doing instead is renewing their minds to focus on growing their personal wealth towards becoming rich. Still, he does not hold out hope that the paradigm shift in the attitudes of both groups that needs to happen will prevent the economic collapse.

Your Key To Saving Your Personal Wealth Is Financial Education

In his conclusion, Robert decides that a great deal of what is occurring to create this financial calamity and collapse lies in our ignorance of financial education. He says that the public is for the most part illiterate financially. Because of this, if you are in the minority that possesses a sound financial education, then you already have a big advantage over the others.

Robert says that this broad financial education gives you a truly unfair advantage over the vast majority of those who do not have one. Using such a grounded financial education, you are able to employ taxes, inflation, debt, and retirement planning. This is supposed to help you to grow wealthy instead of poor.

You can not argue with Robert's reasoning about the ignorance of financial education in the United States. It is no stretch to see it as a significantly contributing factor in the financial collapse. The political establishment has been capable of plundering American's wealth as a result of it.

Suggestions for Saving Your Wealth

Robert suggests that you take proactive steps to strengthen and ultimately save your personal finances. He is not out promoting 401k types of retirement plans. He does have a system of Cash Flow quadrants that he suggests you work in. These are E, B, S, and I. They stand for Employee, Big business owner, Self employed, and Investor.

More than this, Robert suggests that you minimize your tax burden as you are expanding your business. You should leverage your possessions in order to acquire inexpensive access to money via debt. Maybe most importantly, you should invest at least a portion of your assets into items that protect you from the coming hyperinflation, such as gold and silver.

Robert's book "Rich Dad's Conspiracy of the Rich" proves to be a terrific read that has an insightful explanation for the reasons that the economic collapse is far from over. It makes a convincing case that it is actually more likely to get progressively far worse. He turns the somber subject more positive by providing a number of solid ideas for the best means of saving your wealth from the hard times that lie in America's and your future.

The Wealth Mindset - From Pleasure To Contribution

When you think about the differences between rich and poor, a number of contrasting attitudes make them worlds apart from each other. One of the more interesting separations lies in the attitude of the wealth mindset.

You will come to understand what this wealth mindset is, and what the two extremes are that each of the two groups embrace, in the following paragraphs.

The Wealth Mindset Defined

The wealth mindset refers to the attitude you take towards everything in your life. The way that you see your life's purpose and point are a big part of this.

Another way of putting it is what do you want to get out of life, or what legacy do you want to leave behind after your time on this earth is over? All of these concepts dramatically impact a person's attitude towards making money. Their drive to do it is intertwined closely with their concepts of the purpose and meaning of being wealthy.

The Wealth Mindset of the Poor

The wealth mindset of the poor is fairly easily explained by the following short story. A philosopher went around asking people what they would do if they suddenly had a million dollars. One tired working man's response was nothing, he would do absolutely nothing. This is the way that the poor often think. They are looking for a ticket to easy street, a way to not have to do anything that they do not want. To them, wealth represents an escape from the troubles, pain, and problems of life.

The poor and even middle class also operate out of a mindset of fear. They hope that they can keep from losing something. You have heard these types of people say they hope that they do not fail. Similarly, the words they will give it a try come from their mouths more often than they will go and accomplish something. Their mentality is one of defensiveness, of holding onto what they have and not letting it get away from them, or be taken from them.

The poor also do not see a purpose in life much beyond getting by. They are interested in taking their share of happiness out of life. What can life do for them is always in the corner of their minds. These people are not interested in achieving something. You do not hear them making plans to change the world, improve other people's lives, or leave any kind of lasting legacy behind and beyond themselves. They dream of winning the lottery, a sweepstakes like Publisher's Clearinghouse, or a game show like the Price is Right or Wheel of Fortune.

The poor are aiming at achieving very little, and this is exactly what they hit ninety-nine percent of the time. Dreams of gaining wealth are present, but not for any meaningful purpose.

A life of pleasure and of ease is what the poor desire, and it proves to be the end result in most of the few instances where they do succeed enough at something to become wealthy.

If you look at the majority of professional athletes as an example, you begin to understand where they go wrong. The overwhelming majority of them start out as admirable characters. They find at a young age that they have a talent in a particular sport. With some sincere dedication to the sport, they excel enough to reach the top ranks of football, basketball, or baseball. Lucrative contracts for their few peak performance years result. They have achieved wealth, but their poor mindset immediately sets about destroying their accomplishments.

Most of these athletes from humble backgrounds begin living a party and pleasure filled life. They run through their millions or even tens of millions as fast as they are making it. By the time they reach twenty-five to thirty years of age, their professional careers are over. You may have heard the sobering statistic that says it all. Within five years of the end of their professional careers, ninety percent of all such athletes are right back at where they started, with absolutely nothing left to their names. This is the saddest possible testament to the the pleasure filled wealth mindset.

The Wealth Mindset of the Rich

Contrast all of these wealth mindsets of the poor with those of the rich. When you think of the rich, you do not think of lazy people taking it easy. Take Donald Trump as an example. He is a billionaire that is greatly admired by countless Americans. When you read his book, "Trump: Think Like a Billionaire," you see characteristics that the rich have in common.

Trump and the majority of the rich do not slow down and take it easy just because they have achieved great wealth and success.

Far to the contrary, the man does not every take a vacation, unless he is on a working vacation, like playing golf with clients in Florida. To the wealthy, riches lead to more work, not relaxation and ease. Many of the people who work the longest hours in America are exactly those who do not have to because of their financial position, but instead choose to. How many wealthy people do you hear of slowing down in retirement?

Their attitudes towards wealth and money are similarly the opposite of the poor and middle class mentality of fear of losing or failing. The wealthy engage in the game of making money to win and to succeed. They focus on success with an almost reckless abandon. This is not to say that you see the wealthy acting with a rash or fearless mindset. Instead, you see a group of people who look at making money and building up wealth by first looking carefully at the possibilities, then coming to a considered decision, committing to their course of action, then standing behind the decision in order to see it through. They focus on success; they dwell on it. This is what they achieve in the end, and many times sooner rather than later.

The wealthy see a greater purpose in their lives than only making money as well. The rich are ultimately thinking about ways that they can serve others and contribute meaningfully to society. Rewards for these new products, services, and inventions that they create for the benefit of everyone come to them. They are mostly monetary and financial in nature.

This principal of contribution is a key component of the wealth mindset of the rich. They are looking to make a positive impact on the world while they are here.

Steve Jobs is a terrific example of this type of person. He made millions of dollars with his popularizing the personal computer in the 1970's through Apple. After he was divested of the company, he did not sit back and enjoy his success. He went on to create other products that entertained and served the cause of advancing technology.

Pixar, his revolutionary brainchild in animation advanced the field to new heights in the 1990s. His return to Apple in the last ten years has given you such amazing new products as the tiny computer chip driven music storage device the iPod, smart phone iPhone, and most recently the iPad miniature computer.

The rich are also interested in leaving a legacy of accomplishment after they are gone. They do not think about only enriching themselves for their own pleasure and benefits. They give huge portions of their wealth away to help the less fortunate. You can look at Warren Buffet, the legendary Oracle of Omaha, as an example. Called by many the most successful investor in American history, he has given away more than half of his money to the Gates Foundation to help out the poor. Now that is the mindset of a life worth living.

Mindset

RETIREMENT

"Planing for Financial Freedom"

Why You Receive Only a Chunk of Your Retirement Benefit

Remember the Studebaker?

Individuals employed by Studebaker suffered personal loss including the disappearance of their pensions when the plant closed in 1963. However, like many tragedies, their loss created national awareness about the weaknesses of the existing pension system and receives credit for spawning decades of regulations intended to prevent a similar situation from occurring again.

Origin of Qualified Plans

When the Studebaker plant closed, thousands of employees lost their entire pension or received only a fraction of the benefit they had earned. By 1974, legislation known as the *Employee Retirement Income Security Act* of 1974 (ERISA) was passed by Congress with the intent of protecting the retirement benefits of employees.

This new legislation passed regulations creating *Qualified Retirement Plans*. In order for deposits to a retirement plan to qualify for a tax deduction, employers had to take specific steps when funding the plan. This legislation also created explicit nondiscrimination rules and enforceable legal rights for the Participants.

Employers were not required to offer a plan, but when offered, the employer was required to comply with all the requirements of the ERISA regulations. These provisions offset the bulk of the factors that created the Studebaker tragedy.

Defined Benefit Plans

The common retirement plan at that time was a defined benefit plan, which means the plan guaranteed each participant a specific (defined) benefit when upon retirement. The usual factors used in calculating the retirement amount were the employee's salary averaged over a specified number of years, an anticipated interest rate and the number of years of service a participant worked.

Perhaps two of the most distinctive aspects of these plans were that the employer bore the burden of investment downturns and that retirement benefit payments were usually in the form of an annuity from an insurance company. The total participant benefit transferred to an insurance company that then calculated a periodic payment based on participant and spouse life expectancy, and then issued regular monthly or quarterly installment checks.

In other words, if your employer offered a defined benefit plan and the investments lost money for any reason, including a stock market collapse, your employer would be required to make an additional deposit to the plan. Each year the employer would have to increase contributions as necessary to make sure there was enough money to cover your entire retirement benefit. Upon retirement, you would receive a check each month or quarter in a set amount. The amount would never change and you could rely upon it for your budget planning.

Defined Contribution Plans

By the time of ERISA, an alternative type of retirement plan known as a defined contribution plan began increasing in popularity. In this plan design, only the employer is only required to define the annual contribution; there were no guaranteed payments upon retirement. Most of these plans base contributions solely on the participant salary for the current year.

In addition, these plans were not required to use an annuity form of benefit payment, and were ultimately discouraged from including insurance options. In their place, participants primarily receive one-time lump sums or periodic installment payments.

While an installment payment is similar to annuity in that each payment amount would be the same, the base underlying the installments is no longer a guaranteed benefit, and so as depreciation reduces the value of the base, the number of years of the installment payments could reduce as well. The ultimate, if unintended, effect of these plan designs was to mitigate the improvements of ERISA and return some of the risk of the pre-ERISA plans.

If you worked for an employer with a defined contribution plan, regulations required certain steps to ensure any contribution made in a particular year was fair. However, if the investments in the Plan experienced realized or unrealized depreciation, you and the other participants experienced the loss, and you received a reduced retirement benefit.

As the investments depreciate, your installment payments would simply cease earlier than expected. Of course, if the investments appreciate you also share in the in earnings and your retirement benefit would increase. The primary difference is that defined contribution plans provide uncertain retirement benefits.

Not surprisingly, for many companies the primary reason for offering retirement plans became the benefit to the companies such as corporate tax deductions or employee retention, rather than a focus on providing a source of retirement income for the employee. The dominant retirement plans began to shift from *Defined Benefit Plans* to *Defined Contribution Plans*.

401(k) Plans

Around 1978, this change accelerated as a new plan design feature was ferreted out of Internal Revenue Code section 401(k). This section of the code allowed *Defined Contribution Plans* to let the participants make pre-tax deposits towards their retirement benefit. Eventually, the participants also received the ability to make elections and direct how to invest the money that came out of their paycheck.

Originally, 401(k) plans presented an opportunity for employees to supplement the amount of retirement money the employer was providing, thus improving the standard of living they could anticipate at retirement. These plans also encouraged the employee to be aware of and take an active part in retirement planning. However, too swiftly this feature became a way for an employer to further reduce the annual employer contribution instead of provide a benefit for the employee.

Why Your Retirement Funding Is At Risk

Many companies today offer plans where the only contribution is the 401(k) pre-tax salary deductions made by the participants.

When the primary retirement benefit is essentially participant-driven, employees are subject to a type of double jeopardy with regard to successfully funding their retirement benefit.

First, the economic turmoil of the last few years resulted in many employees losing their jobs, and therefore they are unable to contribute to their retirement. For those who remain employed, many are encountering extremely challenging expenses, and have elected to stop contributing.

Meanwhile the second funding risk is actively exacerbating the first. As the participant is bearing the burden of all investment depreciation, the account balance dramatically dwindles in down markets. In most plans, each participant has a segregated account for which he or she is responsible for selecting investments and receiving the investment gain or loss.

In 2008 - 2009, numerous accounts experienced double-digit depreciation and the participant's retirement expectations atrophied. Without ongoing deferral contributions, such losses take significantly longer to rebuild, and substantially reduce base retirement benefits.

The net result is that your retirement account is now at risk of experiencing investment reversals and you are at risk of entering retirement without the funds on which you planned. While the market significantly fluctuates, you could end up receiving only a percentage of your original retirement benefit.

After years of regulatory gyrations, retirement plans arguably have come full circle. Much of the risk so vividly depicted by the pre-ERISA Studebaker closure is back; it just embodies a sleek new model.

ECONOMY

"Managing Resources for Prosperity"

Aftershock - The Next Phase Of The Financial Meltdown

When you hear the expression Aftershock, you likely immediately think of what follows one of these devastating earthquakes that have plagued the world consistently over the last year. Aftershock is more than a tremor that afflicts an earthquake ravaged zone though. It is the book that is shaking the prevailing wisdom that the world of finance has in fact turned the corner following the Great Recession.

About Aftershock and its Authors Credentials

Aftershock: Protect Yourself and Profit in the Next Global Financial Meltdown is the sequel to the best selling and frighteningly prescient book by David Wiedemer and Robert Wiedemer that was entitled America's Bubble Economy: Profit When It Pops and that was published back in 2006, less than a year before the housing, credit, and financial markets collapse whose effects are still affecting you today.

The authors in this previous work explained that America's economy is actually comprised these days of six overinflated bubbles that included housing, the stock market, consumer debt, discretionary spending, the government debt, and the foreign supported U.S. dollar. They forecast the fall of all of these bubbles in time with disastrous consequences.

Lo and behold, you have watched in horror as the first four bubbles catastrophically popped and took your investments, your retirement, your home value, and possibly even your job down with them.

These authors saw all of this coming. Now the bad news is that they are confident that we are only a year or two away from the greatest and remaining two bubbles crashing and burning as well. What will happen when this occurs is the subject of the majority of this upsetting but highly plausible book. You need to be aware of what it has to say. Your entire financial future could depend on it.

Before they get into the heart of their argument, the Wiedemer brothers go through great lengths to make the argument that they are neither gold bugs, bears, or bulls, stock detractors or stock boosters, or currency promoters.

They wholeheartedly say that they are not gloom and doom crusaders or out pushing political ideology or agendas. Their track record in the prior and most recent crash is impressive, as they point out. Their housing bubble crash prediction led to the stock market bubble, then the consumer debt bubble, and finally the consumer discretionary spending bubbles all popping as a result.

Premise of the First Part of the book Aftershock

If you read the first part of their newest book Aftershock, then you will get a refresher course on how the housing market blew up and caused the next three bubbles to tank with it. In short, the authors saw numerous problems in the constantly rising housing prices.

The idea that had become accepted as reality was that housing could only go up in price forever. Because you saw this become the dominant mindset, banks loaned out money that should never have been entrusted to many borrowers. Sub prime loans rose in prominence and frequency, as people who could never hope to re-pay these loans were given them with little justification necessary.

The borrowers were helped into this disaster by the banks. They allowed borrowers three choices for loan payments each month. Principal and interest could be repaid, interest only, or even a part of the interest could be paid. The last option proved to be ruinous as original loans could subsequently rise to one hundred and twen-ty-five percent of the original amount that was borrowed. You heard this called creative financing before it blew up in everyone's faces.

The authors go on to explain how the fall of the housing bubble pulled down the stock market bubble, discretionary spending bub-ble, and consumer debt bubbles. The four of these falling all within a year of each other nearly destroyed the world economy. Unfortu-nately, two bubbles are left to fall, government debt and the U.S. dollar.

Premise of the Second Part of the Book Aftershock

In the next section of the book, the authors proceed to explain how the parts of their predictions that are yet to happen will unfold. A crisis of confidence will envelop government debt levels as the U.S. continues to borrow more and more money to try to pump up the already burst bubbles. They will not succeed in this goal, but in the process, they will spark a confidence failure.

Simply put, one day you will see that foreigners perceive the United States has borrowed so much money that it can never possibly hope to repay it. At that point and time, foreigners will begin heading to the exit doors of the U.S. government bond markets. Treasuries and T-bills will start falling in prices as the bond holders begin tripping over each other. None of them will want to be the last ones out of the investments, especially as they see their value sharply declining.

The last bubble, that of the venerable U.S. dollar, will be the final bubble and the most devastating of all of them when it pops. The Wiedemer brothers see this happening as the government debt is collapsing and the foreigners begin repatriating their dollars to their own currencies of Euros, Yen, Pounds, Francs, and Yuan. The dollar value will collapse as a result. Americans will be impoverished and the middle class will be largely wiped out, assuming their remaining predictions come true.

Premise of the Final Part of the Book Aftershock

David and Robert Wiedemer do not leave readers disenchanted without hope. They actually have a number of positive things to say, with surprising calls of action for you to take to safeguard your future and assets.

For one, they recommend that you change job fields to one that will still be around after these last two bubbles burst. They urgently suggest retooling away from construction, retail, and even some government jobs like teaching, as these will all be drastically cut back. They foresee unemployment topping out at over fifty percent, and only such fields as health care, which are essential for life, going on mostly unaffected.

If you can switch over to a field like health care, the Wiedemer brothers say, then you will be better off.

Regarding investments, they also suggest that you put a significant portion of your assets into gold. The two authors say that they do not have any personal affinity for gold, in fact believing it to be a silly store of value. They show their personal distaste for the conventional wisdom on gold's historical role as the ultimate store of value, yet still suggest that it will go sky high.

How high they feel that it will go, they pointedly will not tell you, stating that you will not find them to be credible any longer if they did. They feel that this will be the best way to safeguard and grow your wealth in the days that are coming. Oddly enough, they believe that after some time at these stratospheric prices, that gold will collapse as the ultimate bubble and finally settle around $60 per ounce.

The authors' time frame for all of this is critical. They believe it will happen sometime between 2010 and 2012 at the latest. In the meantime, they suggest that you start to transition your investments away from stocks, bonds, real estate, and other volatile items that they see turning to ash.

These are sober warnings, but as they come from authors with a dead on track record from the last crash, and their reasoning makes imminent sense, you might be well served to listen to them and to at least take some of their suggestions to heart in order to protect yourself.

What Is Hyperinflation And Can It Happen In The US?

You have probably heard the term hyperinflation thrown around before, especially in recent years.

With all of the money printing that the United States has engaged in since the Great Recession and accompanying financial collapse occurred in 2007, it has become a topic that you are hearing increasingly discussed on the news and financial channels.

The whole subject of hyperinflation is addressed, along with the possibilities of it coming to the United States in the next few years, in the paragraphs that follow.

Hyperinflation Defined and Explained

Hyperinflation is simply defined as an inflation that has become so extremely high that it is no longer under control. This leads to a situation where the prices in the country that is afflicted continue to rise, and quickly, as the currency continues to drop in value.

The media has various definitions for hyperinflation. These range from a subsequent three year inflation rate that nears one hundred percent, to inflation that is greater than fifty percent per month. At the same time, you find that many scholars use the term for rates that are significantly lower, such as double digit inflation in a single year.

166

Actual Causes of Hyperinflation

The actual causes of hyperinflation will probably frighten you, as they hit close to home in the present day United States. The principal cause of hyperinflation is literally an enormous and fast paced increase of the money supply.

This increasing money supply happens as there is no supporting comparable growth rate in services and goods output in the country in question, or there is even a negative growth in such output. What you see result is a forming imbalance between the amount of money supply available and the demand for both the hard currency and deposits in the bank.

Next a total failure of confidence in the country's monetary units happens. You might liken this to a run on a bank, but on a national scale. Government responds by creating price controls and legal tender laws in an effort to stop the drop of the value of the paper money in price comparison to hard currency like gold or silver, and to other commodities. Unfortunately, such measures do not succeed in restoring confidence in the paper money that does not have any intrinsic value besides a shattered faith and trust in the issuing government.

Such hyperinflation often spins into a vicious cycle as a result. When the money issuing agency continues to encourage excessive creation of money, the hyperinflation keeps going. Finally, the group that handles the printing of the national currency is literally unable to print such paper currency at a quicker pace than the rate at which it is dropping. This cancels out their efforts to stimulate the failing economy.

How Inflation Becomes Hyperinflation

You can also see regular hyperinflation similarly develop as a result of behind the scenes problems in an economy and government finance. When the monetary authorities do not pay for rising government expenses from either taxes, cost cutting, or increasing the government debt level, such hyperinflation occurs.

This can happen for one of several reasons. Either government debt no longer finds enough buyers at fair market prices, or taxes collected fall far below the level necessary level to fund the government's expenses, or the two things happen in concert. Whatever the reasons for the rise of hyperinflation, the results are tragic for an economy, country, and people like you.

Examples of Hyperinflation

Hyperinflation commonly affects paper money since it is so easy to boost this form of money supply. All that you have to do is put a few more zeros on to the plates and print these new denomination notes. History is rife with examples of hyperinflation that has hit a number of different countries. In the end, such countries went back to a system of hard money to stop the vicious cycle.

The most classic examples of hyperinflation include Germany following World War I, Hungary after the conclusion of World War II, and Yugoslavia as the country was beginning to break up in the late 1980's. Even the United States has already been a victim of this on more than one occasion in the past.

German Weimar Republic Hyperinflation

In the tail end of 1923, Weimar Republic Germany had resorted to printing two trillion Mark bills. You similarly saw them issuing fifty billion mark postage stamps. The Weimar Republic Reichsbank topped off their hyperinflation by issuing a one hundred trillion Mark bank note.

At this horrific peak when a German man literally took a full wheel barrow's worth of money to the market to buy a loaf of bread, one U.S. dollar purchased four trillion German Marks.

Understandably, Germany has been paranoid about returning to money printing policies that failed them so miserably in the past, even as the U.S. has attempted to goad them into it in the name of saving the international economy.

Post World War II Hungary Hyperinflation

Hungary claims two hyper-inflationary records of dubious distinction. Following the conclusion of World War II in 1946, they printed the largest single denomination banknote ever circulated. It amounted to one hundred quintillion pengő.

They also achieved the record rate of monthly inflation at almost forty-two quadrillion percent in July, 1946. At this rate, the country's prices were doubling literally each thirteen and a half hours. To put this in perspective, Zimbabwe, the African country that is the latest example of hyperinflation run wild, only sees its prices double every five days.

United States Hyperinflation Periods

It may come as a shock to you, but the United States has already experienced three hyper inflationary periods in its brief two hundred and thirty-five year history. During the Revolutionary War and the Civil War, the country recorded significant inflation levels, in particular in the Confederate States of the South.

The United States federal government has also been guilty of debasing the coinage, which led to hyperinflation. President Roosevelt deliberately reducing the amount of gold that the dollar could be exchanged for by fifty percent in 1933 is the most classic example of this. You similarly saw the coinage reduced from ninety-percent silver to less than ten percent silver after 1964, in an effort to save money in the creation of the American coinage.

A Near Future Hyperinflation Scenario in the United States

Now that you know that the U.S. has already suffered from hyperinflation in at least three instances in the last three centuries, it should no longer come as a shock to you that we may be headed for it again in the near future. You find this to be the case because of the enormous amounts of money that were created literally out of thin air and injected into the United States economy since 2007.

The last days of the final George W. Bush administration and the first year of the Obama administration saw the U.S. dollar base increased by in excess of three hundred percent. All of this occurred when the economic output was actually contracting, and not merely growing at a substantially smaller pace than the accompanying money supply.

The law of supply and demand tells you that there will shortly be substantially too many dollars chasing way too few goods. This remains the classic definition of inflation. Will the hyperinflation in the United States grow to match the three hundred percent increase in the base money supply, or merely reach the double digits as a result?

Time will tell if things really get so bad in the States that major unrest and widespread poverty become the norms, particularly for those unfortunate retirees living on fixed incomes.

Why Inflation Is A Monetary Currency Driven Event

If someone were to ask you what is inflation, you might have an answer ready for them. You might say it is things getting more expensive in terms of a fixed dollar value.

But if the same person asked you what causes inflation, you would likely have a hard time giving them a coherent answer. This would not be your fault.

Inflation is terribly misunderstood in the world today. Inflation is actually a monetary, currency driven event.

Correct Definition of Inflation

The truth is that inflation is often incorrectly interpreted in today's pop culture. You, like many people, are likely to consider it to be simply prices going higher. This is not strictly correct though. The actual dictionary definition of inflation turns out to be a substantial and persistent rise in the underlying levels of prices that pertains to a increasing amount of the available quantity of money and leads to the decline in the value of the currency.

Simply put, this means that overall rising prices must be driven up as a result of a increasing supply of money.

Look at the following example to better understand what is and what is not actually inflation. If the Fed increases the supply of American money by two fold, and this causes gasoline prices to subsequently rise the same two fold, then this is inflation, and even hyperinflation at that. This inflation results from a greater quantity of dollars actually competing against one another for the identical supplies of gasoline, which leads to the typical price of gasoline running away.

But if instead, a terrible tragedy were to befall Saudi Arabia, and their oil and gasoline supplies went totally offline as a result, then gasoline prices might similarly double. This would be a terrible event for you and everyone else, not to mention the Saudis, but it would not have any relation to inflation. Because you saw supply cut back drastically, all the while demand stayed the same, prices rose sharply. Here you have two vastly different events that led to the identical end result. Only the first of the two is actually inflation. Inflation is a monetary, currency driven event.

How Supply and Demand Inflation Affects Prices

The truth is that the costs of literally every good or service come from a complex combination of both the supply and demand surrounding the item in question, as well as the supply and demand surrounding the underlying money itself. Some price increases really are based on the supply and demand drivers underlying a commodity.

Inflation though is always driven by a supply and demand set of factors surrounding the currency. The fact that there are two different elements underlying increases in price, or decreases in costs for that matter, makes the whole subject of inflation confusing. It also demonstrates why it is so difficult to actually measure inflation.

The Real Causes of Inflation

When you examine the actual causes of inflation, it helps to understand the complicated subject and how it can affect you personally. Money supplies growing at a more rapid pace than the economy that underlies them actually leads to inflation. Consider inflation to be smoke, and the causes of it to be the fire that creates it.

If inflation is the smoke, then the excess creation of new money is the fire that leads to it. It is also helpful for you to remember than when a fire first flares up brightly, you might not witness any smoke immediately. You can be sure that there will be smoke, and plenty of it, if this fire continues to burn brighter and hotter.

The Controller of the Money Supply

Another misconception in popular culture today is that banks are able to expand the money supply through offering credit and making loans. This is a common misnomer. Only the central bank of a country is able to literally impact the base supply of money. Banks creating credit is not really new money. Credit is really only the ability to use another person or organization's money.

As an example, if a person offered to give you a one hundred thousand dollar check as a no strings attached gift, you would get wildly excited. If the individual instead offered you the identical hundred thousand dollars in the form of a loan, then you would not get so excited. This is to say that money and credit turn out to be two entirely different things. It is similarly true that while credit expansion does not equate to overall inflation, credit contraction does not signify that there is an underlying deflation at work.

Finding the Coming Inflation

You often hear it whispered these days that a mountain of inflation lies ahead. If this is the case, that there will be a significant amount of inflationary smoke in the near future, then you should consider the underlying fire that will cause this. This is the U.S. Federal Reserve's money supply policies and data of the recent years. These statistics can be examined from a variety of different angles.

Money of Zero Maturity

Money of zero maturity, or MZM, is a good place to look. This phrase simply means all money, including currency, savings accounts, checking accounts, and money market accounts. It does not consider certificates of deposit or other time sensitive deposits.

In the middle of the first decade of 2000, this MZM growth lay stable at around the growth of the Consumer Price Index, or CPI, government released measure of inflation. They were both averaging approximately three percent in both 2004 and 2005. Before the middle of 2006, the CPI typically moved in almost lock step with the MZM increase. As MZM rates expanded, the CPI did the same.

Everything changed radically in 2006, leading to an as of yet not rectified disconnect between the MZM and CPI inflation rate. These events will be familiar to you and almost all readers. They were the subprime mortgage melt down of 2007, the overall credit crunch later the same year, and the worldwide stock crash that happened early in 2008.

The Fed responded with the only way that it really could with its limited power base, by cranking up the fire, or printing press. Under Ben Bernake's leadership, they radically grew the monetary base.

Having stood at only four percent per year when Bernake came to be Chairman of the Federal Reserve, this annual rate of MZM growth skyrocketed to eight percent, then twelve percent, then sixteen percent by 2008.

The Fed flooded the system with brand new Fiat paper dollars. Since just the start of 2008, the Fed has grown the MZM at a radical level that some weeks amounted to nearly thirteen percent. This is an astonishing rate that has led to a dollar money supply increase of over three hundred percent since 2007.

What This Massive Growth of the Money Supply Means for You Personally

Going back to the smoke and fire analogy, the fires of monetary expansion have been working overtime. So far, you have not seen the accompanying smoke demonstrated much of anywhere except for in commodities prices.

You can be sure that the correlations between money supply and inflation will hold true, as they always do. Look for sharply higher prices in the near future, either at once, or over a longer period of still painful years. This will likely affect everything from food, to electronics, to clothes, to durable goods like washing machines.

If you are looking for an easy way to protect yourself from the imminent inflation threat, you can invest a part of your money into hard commodities such as gold, silver, and even real estate. These will increase at the same rate or faster than the underlying inflation does, especially as other people begin piling their monies into such commodities in order to protect it.

The End of Prosperity - Prepare For More And Higher Taxes

You may or may not be aware of the book that three respected men wrote on the eve of the critical 2008 presidential elections entitled The End of Prosperity. This work proves to be just as relevant today as it was before President Obama got elected and began his attempt to transform the United States into a socialist styled welfare state.

"The End of Prosperity: How Higher Taxes Will Doom the Economy - If We Let It Happen" investigates many critical issues at the forefront of public policy debates to this very day. You do not have to be on one side of the political spectrum or the other to appreciate its important authors and their sweeping and powerful conclusions.

The Authors of The End of Prosperity

The father of supply side economic theory, who was an important member of the Economic Policy Advisory Board of President Reagen, is Arthur Laffer. In this work, he teamed up with The Wall Street Journal's editorial board member Stephen Moore and Peter J. Tanous, a respected investment adviser. These prestigious and experienced authors wanted to get a series of messages out to the American public.

The Premise of The End of Prosperity

The main premise of the book revolved around a stark choice that faced the American public in the critically important election of 2008. The authors wished for you and all Americans to be aware of the fact that our exceptionally high standard of living stood in serious jeopardy. They feared that the economic strength that had made America the idol of the rest of the world for its strongly pro growth policies of the past twenty-five years was in danger of being decidedly and irrevocably reversed by a new president with very different economic ideas.

Background to The End of Prosperity

The three authors point out very clearly that the U.S. has been basking in an unprecedented light of prosperity since the early 1980's. This economic boom proved to be unrivaled in history for the numbers of new jobs created, the resulting wealth explosion, and finally the higher standards of living for all Americans.

During the terms of both Presidents Ronald Regan and Bill Clinton, the entire incentive structure of the country was altered, especially regarding regulation, inflation, and taxes. You saw the end result revealed, a national economy that rose seemingly from the ashes of the crushing inflation and stagnant, poor growth of the decade of the 1970's to lead the entire world.

The authors make a good case in point about how the whole rest of the world has followed the economic leader, the United States, in this. The example of greater levels of economic freedom, lower rates of taxes, and sound monetary policies have been taken to heart and adopted by both other developed and developing nations alike.

Ironically, they say, only one nation is in fact turning away from such successful policies of growth, thereby putting your future and the country's prosperity both at risk. This country is the United States.

Purpose of the Book The End of Prosperity

Even though what the authors feared most has come to pass with the elections of President Barack Obama and Speaker of the House Nancy Pelosi, the book still offers many valuable insights and warnings for today. The goal of authors Laffer, Moore, and Tanous may have been to present convincing factual evidence that they hoped all Americans would seriously consider before going out to vote.

This relevant information centered around how the United States achieved such prosperity that is now taken completely for granted. They were worried that radical new policies would snuff out the U.S. track record of leading growth around the world and creating jobs like a proverbially well oiled machine.

Their message that is still relevant is for you and all Americans to place a high and cherished value on the country's much envied and copied free enterprise system. They aim to teach the ways that Americans can strive to safeguard their individual investments during the coming storms created by radical new economic policies.

Main Points of The End of Prosperity

The Laffler Curve that the first of the authors is famed for inventing is discussed at some length in the book. This idea of his states that those who are given incentives to work hard will respond to these incentives.

Simply put, if a person took $4 out of your paycheck for every $10 you earned, would you have much incentive to work hard? The idea behind the curve is how would a person respond to $5 or $6 for every $10 being taken out. It states that at some point of high taxation, you actually see government revenues decrease, even though tax rates are rising.

The book questions how fair it is to gang up on the wealthy. They remind you that the highest one percent of income earners literally pay a full forty percent of all the taxes that the government collects. And this goes on while the lowest earning fifty percent pay a mere three percent of the tax burden.

As tough as the present economic situation is, the book points out, it will only get worse if the wealthy are ganged up on in a quest for equality and fairness. The authors make a very good point in demonstrating that the likes of leaders such as Steve Jobs, Bill Gates, and Michael Dell have all helped to make every American's world better. Without them and their initiatives to create, design, invent, and build, today you would not have any laptop computers, Amazon.com, or iPod.

This only happened as brave entrepreneurs were able to reap what they sowed. These captains of industry do not put in long, tiring hours making the world better so that they can enrich the government. They work hard to improve themselves and to contribute to society and the world. That is the entire point of the book The End of Prosperity.

Bi-Partisan Nature of The End of Prosperity

Although you may think that this is a heavily right leaning book, it is actually not the case. In fact, it is a greatly bi-partisan book. It is a work that gives President Bill Clinton some of the credit for the economic expansion of the twenty-five years of the eighties and nineties. It takes a heavily centrist position and cuts across traditional political party lines.

The book uses historical events and other factual data, not political perspective, faith, or dogmatic ideas. As an example of this, the authors took issue with four presidents. Two of them were Republicans like Richard Nixon and Gerald Ford. Two of them were democrats like Lyndon B. Johnson and Jimmy Carter.

The fourth chapter, entitled Honey, We Shrank the Economy, examines their various misguided economic policies, along with the accompanying results that followed. This chapter does not cut any president a break, regardless of political party affiliation. Instead, it thoroughly discredits both the failed Democratic and Republican policies of their days.

This sample chapter also is filled with numerous thought provoking and idea challenging quotes. You may decide to like them or violently disagree with them, but the authors will certainly make you think about your preconceived notions of what makes the U.S. economy so great.

5 Reasons Why Obama Continues To Cripple The Economy

President Obama was elected on promises of hope and change. His first year and a half of administration has talked a lot about such hope and change but only affected policies that are actually killing the economy.

In the following paragraphs, you will read five different reasons that the President who promised so much during the epic campaign is only making the present situation worse.

He is Creating Excessive New Debt

President Obama's predecessor President George W. Bush had numerous critics who accused him of resorting to the creation of a significant and scary amount of debt during his two terms. But under the newest president, it has taken him less than two years to raise the debt more than President Bush did in eight years.

You have watched the national debt under President Obama grow to more than $14 trillion dollars and rising. Between his increased social spending and new health plan, another trillion dollars or more are projected to be added to the debt in the next several years. Based on the projected budgets' spending for the next four to eight years and the still declining tax base, overspending will raise the national debt still another one to two trillion dollars between now and 2015 - 2020.

This excessive new debt is beginning to weigh on the economy in a number of ways. Foreign investors are more wary about purchasing U.S. debt and investments as a result of it. The interest payments on the debt are similarly taking up a larger and greater share of the Federal budget every year. When the interest rates for the government rise, as the invariably must eventually with the constant creation of unmanageable debt, these rising interest payments will become a serious problem for government services and the whole economy.

He is Listening to and Following the Fed's Bad Advice

Obama is not entirely to blame for the poor policies that he is enacting so far as President. He has a variety of well respected economists and policy makers who are feeding him poor and even dangerous economic advice.

Chief among these is Ben Bernake at the Federal Reserve Board. Mr. Bernake has been nicknamed Helicopter Ben in the past because of his belief that if the U.S. economy ever got into real trouble, the problems could be simply solved if a person had a large enough helicopter to fly around the country throwing money out of it to the people. This would be done, he believed, in order to keep the consumer spending machine running at a fast clip.

As a result of the momentous economic events that have shaken the national economy in the past few years, Helicopter Ben Bernake has gained the motive for recommending these policies of spraying money created out of thin air in all directions. Chairman Bernake could not do this without the consent of the President, who recently reappointed him to another term.

Besides probably creating runaway inflation in the near future to severely hamstring the economy, the policies of the Fed are leading the newest president to other poor choices as well.

He Supports the Banking System to a Fault

While at first this may sound like a good idea, President Obama has taken supporting the banking system too far. You know by now that the banks bore a lion's share of the blame in the causes of the Great Recession and financial collapse. Many thought that the new president would take a hand to better regulate the banks, as well as to make them help pay to repair the damage that they caused to the economy.

Instead, the president, encouraged by members of the Federal Reserve like Ben Bernake, has basically backed off of his pledge to regulate and tax the banks for the disaster. Instead of letting banks fail that proved to be more involved in the gambling business than in the sound banking business, he has allowed the Treasury and the Fed to backstop their losses and take their bad investments off of their books.

These worthless derivatives and near worthless sub prime loans, or poor loans and investments made during the peak of the boom before the economic crash in 2007-2008, are still with us. No longer on the balance sheets of banks that should have been allowed to fail, these complicated investments are now silently strangling the entire Federal government's balance sheet instead. President Obama's continuing to support the banking system is also killing the economy.

He Supports Wall Street Too Much

The other group that bore a great deal of the blame for the financial crisis turned out to be the major investment firms of Wall Street, such as Morgan Stanley, Goldman Sachs, and the former largest brokerage firm in the world Merrill Lynch.

President Obama also promised to restrict their wildly speculative activities when he took office. Instead, he is allowing them to go back to their speculation and asset inflating activities again unchecked. They are busy selling more packaged structured investments and derivatives now than they did before the earlier crash. This allows them to return to the practices of showing unbelievable gains on investments now at the expense of a future price to pay, so that they can once more pay the large multi million dollar bonuses to all of their mid and high level executives.

While other leaders of European countries such as Great Britain, France, and Germany are taking steps to not let such firms play havoc with the world financial system again, President Obama is not regulating their activities in the U.S. as he promised. Instead he is allowing them to again manipulate the economy. As a result of this, another financial collapse is likely in the cards sometime in the near to medium term future.

He Is Promoting An Excessive War Cost

Whether or not you are morally for or against the wars in Iraq and Afghanistan, you will probably agree that they are ruinously expensive as they continue to drag on. The wars in these two countries are still costing the United States treasury in excess of $1.08 trillion per year in 2010, according to the Center for Defense Information. This is more than eight years after they began.

With the government having to borrow an increasingly larger amount of money every year to finance the budget shortfalls, this is having a severely draining effect on the national budget and the overall economy.

In his lauded campaign, the President repeatedly pledged to bring home the troops from Iraq, and he has actually reduced the number to just over fifty thousand men and women there. But many of these troops have instead been shifted over to Afghanistan to try to beat down the persistent and continuous opposition found in that country. This means that instead of lowering the costs spent on the war every year as he pledged, President Obama has mostly only shifted the theater where your tax money is being spent.

He Has Not Extended The Bush Tax Cuts

Once again, you may agree or disagree with the Bush tax cut policies that the former President enacted years ago. Repealing them now, with the economy still struggling to climb out of the recessionary hole, would be like adding a new tax on to the most productive members of society. Continuing uncertainty over this policy is keeping the wealthy and business owners from feeling confident enough to hire more Americans, thereby reducing the unemployment rate.

Signs Of America's Rapid Fall Into A Third World Country

When you hear the phrase Third World America, it immediately gets your intention. This is exactly what the author Arianna Huffington intends with her new book.

This is not a work about the significant number of poor who live in America today, though it deals with this shocking statistic.

Instead, you will find that this is a book about the current trajectory that the Untied States is on, and the unenviable status that the author believes we will shortly achieve, if we do not take some drastic actions soon.

About the Author Arianna Huffington

The author of Third World America is Arianna Huffington, a women who is at the cutting edge front of news and writing. She is both the author of thirteen books, a nationally syndicated columnist writer, and the editor and co-founder of the Huffington Post.

She is furthermore the co-host of a ratings generating program on public radio called "Left, Right, and Center," that is a political round table formatted program.

As if this were not enough, Arianna Huffington has been named to the list of fifty people who shaped the last decade by the Financial Times, as well as to the Time 100, which proves to be the list of the most influential one hundred people in the world, according to Time Magazine. She is a graduate of Cambridge University with a Masters in Economics and is a native of Greece.

Premise of Third World America

Arianna Huffington starts out with a premise that is hard for you to argue against. She says that the middle class citizens of American have shrunk to an endangered species level. She takes it a step further by arguing that the once grand American Dream that you aspired to, of having a safe, comfortable, and convenient standard of living, has faded away to obscurity. This is her basis for claiming that the United States stands on the threshold of literally turning into a third world nation.

Arianna backs up these claims with a number of points of evidence that she shows are visible all around you. She demonstrates to you how the industrial base is disappearing, along with the sorts of jobs that have underlain the strength of the economy for in excess of one hundred years. She furthermore holds up the education system that is a wreck. This will make it more difficult for the future citizenry to gain the skills and knowledge that it requires to obtain the cutting edged jobs of the twenty-first century.

Arianna has many other weak elements in the United States to pick on in the work. She points to the crumbling infrastructure throughout America too. This includes bridges, roads, electrical systems, transportation networks, water, and sewer systems.

She holds up the economic system that is constantly at the mercy of the avarice and greed of corporations plagued by scandals and most interested in bonus amounts.

Finally, she states that our much envied political system is completely broken, since it has become a slave to the handful of financial power brokers who use their huge sums of money to control both Democrats and Republicans alike.

The Dwindling Middle Class

Arianna Huffington pays special attention to how badly the middle class is dwindling and what a tragedy this is for our country. One out of every six American citizens are involved in programs to combat poverty. Fully fifty million Americans are a part of Medicaid. Forty million different Americans must have food stamps in order to survive. Currently ten million Americans receive unemployment benefits.

Everywhere you look, you see the decline and gradual disappearance of the middle class. Arianna mourns the loss of this middle class, and rightfully so. As she claims, this critical group has separated the United States from third world countries where they are only rich and poor.

America's middle class has been the engine for such a huge portion of the country's political stability and economic success as well. As the rich grow richer, the poor grow poorer, and the middle class vanish, Arianna conjures up the specter of a dark alter ego to the American Dream, an American Nightmare that we have fumbled our way into.

She points out a future that involves a country slipping against its rivals, one where your kids and grand kids will be party to a smaller number of opportunities and enjoy a lesser standard of living than you have now. She paints a bleak picture of an America in decline as the economic, political, and industrial leader of the world.

Third World America's Proactive Solutions

Arianna Huffington's Third World America is not a book totally without hope. As in her last book "Pigs at the Trough," she practices her no holds barred brand of journalism that she has built a reputation on by effectively naming the names of the guilty parties, pointing fingers at those who are responsible for the decline, and sharing the critical information on who is destroying the American Dream.

More importantly than this, you will she that she lays out a road map with step by step directions of what has to be done in order to put a halt to the decline, reverse the damage, and take America off the path of becoming a third world nation.

The Missing Sense of Urgency

A critical element that Arianna says is necessary to save the country is a sense of urgency that the problems are real and must be swiftly addressed. She holds up recent interviews with President Obama as proof of this general disregard for the urgent situation. She recalls the sense of urgency that the country showed, both democrats and republicans, when the financial system was on the verge of collapsing over a weekend two years ago after the financial firm Lehman Brothers went down.

When Wall Street was saved, Arianna claims, it was because all of the disparate players put aside their petty differences to come together and say that you can not allow the entire financial system to fall apart. Even though you may disagree on what will save it from collapse, you have to try everything, since you simply can not afford for it to happen.

This is the sort of necessary urgency that is missing these days. Arianna points out that there have been numerous conversations surrounding jobs and their priority, and how important they will be as a focus of the new President. She says that President Obama says he wants to hear all ideas. Both Republicans and Democrats have been shouting all sorts of ideas ranging from a major jobs and infrastructure program to a payroll tax holiday.

People have suggested an infrastructure bank, a green bank, and even tax credits for smaller businesses. She points out that there are many ideas that have been offered. Despite all of the ideas, the critical sense of urgency, as well as the accompanying political will to actually do something to address the problems, is just not there.

Until it surfaces with some degree of stay in power, Arianna Huffington says things will not get any better regarding the host of problems facing the country and sapping at its middle class base and strength. If you are concerned about the future of the country, then this book is a must read.

Why the Real Unemployment Rate Is Around 20% and Rising

In only the last several years, you have no doubt heard more about the unemployment rate than you want to for the rest of your life. The talking heads and pundits tell you that it peaked out at 10.2 percent back in October of 2009.

They attempt to convince you that this followed from the low rate at the beginning of the Great Recession of 4.4% in March of 2007.

The official statistics tell you that it rose to 6.2% in August of 2008, 8.1% by February of 2009, 9.4% only three months afterward, and then reaching the previously mentioned high of 10.2% in October.

It may surprise you to learn that these are not the actual unemployment numbers though. In fact, when unemployment is measured according to the formula that was used when President Bill Clinton took office, it is actually around 20%. In the following text, you will see how this great disguise of actual unemployment came to be.

The Official Present Rate of Record Unemployment

The currently used official unemployment number paints a picture of unemployment that is the highest that it has been since the 1983 recession. Back then, it peaked above 10% for a long ten months.

Again though, these previous numbers were figured according to a different unemployment rate formula.

The Measure of Unemployment Used Today

Today's formula only counts a narrow segment of the non working population as unemployed. The people who are counted as unemployed do not currently have a job and have seriously attempted to find work over the last four weeks. They are all presently ready and willing to start work. This is called the U3 unemployment rate. It is also defined as the ratio of the civilian labor force that is aggressively seeking work but is still unemployed.

Other Measures of Unemployment

You may have heard the saying that nothing is so convincing as a lie that is hidden within plain sight. Rather than do away with the other measures of unemployment when the formula was changed, the Bureau of Labor Statistics simply buried the real unemployment number in a mountain of other employment data and statistics. These are explained below.

The first measurement is called U1. It is a percentage of the labor force that has been unemployed for at least fifteen weeks or more. This is a straight forward number that does not begin to tell the story of the high unemployment in the U.S today.

U2 is another number released every month. It represents the percentage of the working population that has either lost a job or finished a temporary work assignment. While this is a better number for unemployment, it still leaves out a great number of other would be workers.

The U3 is today's official unemployment rate. It represents those people in the total civilian work force who are unemployed and still seeking to be employed. It is a number that is less than half as high as the unemployment number that was used until after President Clinton took office, and it woefully under reports the serious problem in the present U.S. job market.

The U4 figure is a number that begins to more accurately reflect the current job reality. It includes everyone in the official U3 rate as well as discouraged workers. These are workers who have completely given up seeking employment as a result of feeling like the present economic environment does not offer them good opportunities for finding work. When you add these discouraged workers to the official numbers, it adds several tenths of a full percentage point on to the presently accepted official unemployment rate.

The U5 figure takes the numbers a step closer to real unemployment. This statistic represents U4 workers along with all of the so called marginally attached, or loosely attached, workers. Such marginally attached workers are people who have simply quit looking for work as a result of varying different reasons. Among these workers are those that they feel their efforts to find work would simply be a waste of time.

This attitude moves them into the discouraged worker group. Still others who have additional reasons for not looking for work are actually categorized as the marginally attached. These include people who wish to work and are bodily able to work, but who have not sought out work lately. Tallying them along with the other discouraged workers also adds a few more tents of a percentage point to the presently used official unemployment rate.

Finally, you come to the number that used to represent unemployment in the United States, the U6. U6 stands for all of the U5 people, as well as people who are only working part time. These part timers are also people who state that they would like to have full time work, but can not find it as a result of the present economic climate.

They are also known as the under employed. This is still considered to be the most inclusive and complete measurement of labor market unemployment that the government offers. The only problem with it is that no one pays attention to it seriously anymore. When you add the under employed back into the official unemployment rate number, it increases by several percentage points.

There is still something else going on with the number juggling act that the Bureau of Labor Statistics performs every month. The inclusion of the U4, U5, and U6 worker types is only supposed to increase the official unemployment rate by maybe four or five percentage points. Truthfully, the released U6 number is presently in excess of eighteen percent, while the official unemployment rate is only 9.7%.

What the Real Unemployment Numbers Mean

You can see that if the country was still using the same measure for unemployment that you had when President Clinton took office, the unemployment rate now would stand at around eighteen percent. This means that actual and true unemployment is really about twice the official rate released every month.

Comparing this eighteen percent rate to the recession of 1983, it is substantially higher than the previous recent record high unemployment of just over ten percent.

The real U6 number is an unemployment record going back well before World War II. In fact, it is almost what the unemployment numbers were during the peak of the Great Depression, when they broke twenty percent.

Why the Method for Figuring the Unemployment Rate Was Changed

Bill Clinton was interested in legacies early on in his presidency. By changing the official unemployment formula to sweep away the so called discouraged workers, he attained a record low unemployment level not seen in decades. The reason for his changing the official unemployment calculation formula had a lot to do with "the economy stupid," as he was fond of saying. He wanted the numbers to look better than they actually were.

Why Unemployment Is Actually Still Rising Despite What the Official Rate Claims

As Nouriel Roubini and a number of other prominent economists have claimed, many of the jobs that have been lost in the U.S. are gone for good. Put another, more sobering way, you might say that they are never coming back.

As a result of the Great Recession, many companies have either forcefully increased their employees' operating efficiency or outsourced their jobs to economies where the costs of labor are substantially less than in the United States. As if this were not bad enough news, all of the latest economic data has continued to demonstrate the many ugly signs pointing towards a double dip recession.

The economy has suffered from a dramatic transformation and it will not simply or easily go back to the levels that were seen before 2007. Prepare yourself for the grim, new economic reality.

<u>POLITICS</u>

"Banking and Government Interventions"

Politics

The Financial Wipeout of the American Middle Class

The middle class is being wiped out financially because the infrastructure that supported the middle class has been yanked out from under it. America previously had a very strong middle class and the country was a world leader in all respects manufacturing, scientific discoveries, economic prosperity, high rate of home-ownership, excellent employee benefits and a strong dollar based on the gold standard. The working people of the 1970's had far greater purchasing power than employees have today.

The Downfall of the American Dollar

The erosion of the middle class started discretely in 1971 when the government abandoned the gold standard for a free-floating dollar. Previously, the dollar was pegged at $35 per ounce of gold and this constant value gave true purchasing power to the middle class. With a free-floating dollar, however, the value fluctuates daily and emerging foreign economies forced it into decline. This erosion of value made it more expensive for the middle class to maintain its standard of living so people turned to credit to make up the difference.

The emerging foreign economies were based on manufacturing and, with their new factories and low-wage workers, they were able to manufacture products at a lower cost than their American counterparts.

American corporations saw greater profit in closing their American factories and moving overseas. This move was a further push toward wiping out the middle class, as they now had no jobs to pay their increasing debt. Millions of jobs have permanently left the United States.

The Employment Disaster

As the unemployment rate increased, the demand for the remaining jobs became intense. Employers were able to hire highly educated employees at a low salary. Once employers realized they had the upper hand and no longer had to compete for the top employees, they began to abolish employee benefits.

Pensions were the first benefit to disappear. Men and women were loyal to a company for life, and in exchange the company paid a pension when the employees turned 65 years of age. Now the middle class has to fund its own retirement with the declining dollar, increasing debt load and fewer chances for a decent paying job.

Company-paid health insurance was the next benefit tossed aside. Previously, companies paid the health insurance premium for their employees. The employee simply paid a small supplement of a few dollars a week for family coverage, if he had a family. Otherwise, his health insurance was free. This increased financial strain put further stress on a disappearing middle class in several ways.

Americans, who has previously enjoyed good health and the best medical care in the world, could no longer afford to go to the doctor. As a result, Americans have the worst access to health care in the Western world. They wait until a small problem is a major one and then need expensive hospital care for which they cannot pay. This burden falls on the middle class taxpayer.

Companies traditionally gave a two-week paid vacation to their employees every year since the early 1900's. Today, however, many employees work year-round without ever receiving a vacation. This only benefits the American corporations as they get productivity from the employee for 52 weeks instead of 50 weeks. This put further stress on the health of the middle class because no one can work continuously without a vacation.

Reduced Spending on Education

The declining dollar has reduced spending on education and, as a result, American high school graduates have an inferior education to students in other Western nations. Millions of American students graduate from high school with little more than basic reading and math skills. They have less knowledge than their grandparents do. The result is that Americans are no longer competitive in the global workforce. The emerging foreign economies, however, invested in educating their people and this has caused even more jobs to be permanently lost to our overseas competitors.

The Final Housing Blowout

The final blow to the middle class occurred with the housing crisis. The American dream of owning a home became a nightmare as million of Americans lost the equity in their homes. Today, more than one-half of all mortgages are for a greater amount than the value of the houses.

Millions of homes sit vacant as Americans pack up and leave, walking away from piles of debt that have burdened them beyond comparison. Bankruptcy and foreclosure are at the highest rates in our nation's history, even worse than the Great Depression.

Possible Solutions

The middle class is not completely without power and there are several things that people can do about the financial crisis. The strongest power that the middle class has is at the voting polls. Simply showing up at the polls, however, will not solve the problem. The middle class needs to become politically involved and elect responsible people to Congress.

The middle class needs to demand a return to the gold standard, or at least to a precious metals standard which would include several things besides gold. The dollar will again be very strong when it has a constant value rather than a fluctuating one. The American dollar should not be valued against other countries in the world as it has been shown that a global economy does not function in our best interests.

Although traditional advice is to live below ones means, frequently that is not possible today with so many people living on unemployment or working for minimum wage. However, making every effort to cut expenses and save money will result in a stronger middle class.

Restructuring the family debt to lower the monthly payment can free up some money to build an emergency fund. Savings are the earmark of a strong middle class.

Other things that Americans can do to lower their expenses are to exercise regularly and maintain a normal weight. Obesity and a sedentary lifestyle have caused many Americans to lose their life savings because of the related medical bills.

Recycling is another money-saver. The middle class can cut expenses significantly by using environmentally friendly materials and by recycling household items for other uses.

Reduce the amount of paper products and other disposables, repair instead of replace, and other conservative measures will help to increase the wealth of the middle class.

Putting pressure on lawmakers for a nationwide employee bill of rights will solve many problems in the workplace. Everyone needs a break from working all year. People need a living wage, not minimum wage.

Health care needs to be overhauled to make it affordable for everyone. The middle class can cut expenses on medical care by using medical clinics instead of private physicians, buying generic drugs instead of proprietary, and living a healthy lifestyle with proper diet and exercise.

The Artificial Production of Booms and Recessions

Many people think that economic booms and recessions just happen. They may have some awareness that the interest rate setting of the Federal Reserve has something to do with it, but the concept of the artificial production of booms and recessions by the Fed seems alien to them. Perhaps they have just never heard about this, or perhaps they have just dismissed it.

However the fact is that this indeed seems to be the case. The question of exactly why the Federal Reserve partakes in this kind of cyclical manipulation of the US financial system is a bit more complex. To understand this a bit better we need to look more closely at the Federal Reserve, how it originated, what it is exactly, and what its powers and motivations are.

The History of the Federal Reserve

Central banking in the United States has had a series of stops and starts. In 1791 the First Bank of the United States was established, ratified by Washington at the urging of Alexander Hamilton. Its charter was for 20 years.

James Madison and Thomas Jefferson were strongly opposed to the bank's establishment, believing that centralized banking separate from the U.S. government would give the institution far too much power over the nation's economic well being and affairs. Nevertheless the bank was established and existed until its charter ran out in 1811.

In 1816, though he had opposed the previous bank, James Madison gave the go ahead for the Second Bank of the United States. It again had a 20 year charter, making it up for renewal in 1836. Andrew Jackson was running for reelection in 1832 and was deadly opposed, as were his supporters, to the bank. A large part of his campaign was based on his promise to kill the Second Bank of the United States, which he indeed did. The bank's charter was not renewed and though it attempted to continue as an ordinary private concern, it went bankrupt a short time after this.

The Federal Reserve Bank, the nation's third central bank, was established in 1913 by congressional vote (while many members of congress were absent due to the Christmas holiday), and and the bill responsible for its creation was signed by president Woodrow Wilson. Its purported function was to manage, control and stabilize the monetary flow and economic conditions in the United States. There are many, however, who believe that its real goals were and are not so responsible and public minded.

The Federal Reserve is not a government institution but a private bank, this is another fact little known to many people (though it is coming more and more into public consciousness). Though it claims to have some sort of different status from ordinary banks in the private sector, besides its obvious powers to basically make money out of thin air and to control rates of interest, there is little to fundamentally differentiate it from any other private enterprise.

As such it exists mainly to enrich its own interests rather than serve the American people as it claims. And here we come to the problem with the bank, and the reason many presidents and government officials have historically been opposed to central banking in general: as soon as you have a private, for profit corporation in charge of the money supply of an entire nation, you have a situation that is ripe for all kinds of corruption and mismanagement.

Therefore various individuals and parties in our government have fought a long and recurring battle to abolish these potentially corrupt and self interested institutions. However, other government officials who were allied with large scale bankers have wanted these banks to exist either in exchange for political support or because of actual financial ties with the institutions. Thus, the Federal Reserve has managed to gain the position it now occupies.

The Federal Reserve is a centralized bank with 12 branch banks in districts around the U.S. These satellite FEDs in turn have member banks in the regions in which they are established. The essential reason there is so much legitimate concern about this system is because it is primarily interest/debt based. The FED has the power, established in the original mostly secretly penned Federal Reserve Act of 1913, to create and lend as much money as it wishes without the oversee of the Federal Government.

It can also set and adjust the interest rates on this lent money as it wishes, thus controlling its availability and flow. The FED is a lending institution, and it lends to ordinary banks and to the federal government at interest. This can only mean one thing, an ever mounting debt that banks, other lending institutions, the federal government, and finally U.S. citizens will find harder and harder to pay back.

When one takes the long view, the system is quite absurd. Since the source of the money supply, The Federal Reserve, lends money at interest rather than simply circulating it, a debt cycle that is self perpetuating is created.

Those in charge of the FED are well aware of this, and many believe that they keep it going in order to perpetuate its stranglehold on governments and world affairs. In looking at the boom and bust cycles that punctuate the history of central banking (indeed not just in the US but globally), it's hard to come to any other conclusion.

How the Federal Reserve Creates Artificial Booms and Recessions

The Federal Reserve creates artificial booms and recessions, for its own ends, in the following way: they lower interest rates to levels below what are necessary, encouraging people and businesses to borrow and to make speculative, optimistic investments.

Times seem to be good until the bubble bursts, the investments are not sustainable, demand goes down, the investments lose their worth, and the banks cannot recoup the money they have lent. The FED may attempt to keep the artificial boom going even longer by printing more money (technically the US Treasury actually prints the currency, but this is completely at the discretion of the FED) so that there is a temporary surplus, and lending and borrowing seem to recover.

But this intentional inflation strategy can only go so far and eventually an even larger collapse ensues. Banks themselves are unable to maintain stability, not to mention the average consumer, who now has greater debt and can no longer borrow easily.

Prices often rise as businesses try to fund the costs of production without increasing their borrowing.

Claiming to assist banks to recoup their losses, the FED raises interest rates, discouraging borrowing among all except the wealthy. One might think that the Federal Reserve itself gets hit by the bursting of the bubble, but the net effect of the entire cycle is to increase the power of the FED to appropriate what it wishes for itself and increase its hold on the economy. In the name of bailouts it assists large corporations it favors and can concentrate wealth in the hands of a small elite.

To put it bluntly, the whole thing is an inside job, at least in the view of critics of the system, and it is hard to argue with this conclusion when one looks at the facts. The Federal Reserve is not working in the interests of stabilizing the economy, but rather managing boom and bust cycles to consolidate its power and to gradually deprive the average citizen of financial freedom, borrowing and buying power, and resources. What's really at issue here is power to control. Those who have control can make vast amounts of money, and by extension, force entire governments and peoples to do their bidding.

This may seem like something of a nightmare scenario. However, frankly discussing it is the first step toward change. People need to know the stark reality of the fairly ignorant forces at work here. This in itself can initiate a new sort of sociological phase. One in which individuals feel free to both think more realistically (as well as creatively) about their financial endeavors and investments, and in which cooperation on community and state levels in a mutually helpful manner becomes more and more the norm.

Behind all this, if one looks closely, one finds philosophies, ways of thinking, and indeed whole world views. The debt based system is fundamentally an expression of human greed and ignorance. It is a new mind set of realism, egalitarianism, creative solutions, and more enlightened behavior that will ultimately turn everything around.

The Debt Virus - A Radical Economic Reorganization

Originally published in 1992 by Jacques S. Jaikara, M.D., "Debt Virus: A Compelling Solution to the World's Debt Problems" questions the traditional role of money in our economy. Even more relevant today due to the substantial amount of the national debt and people's growing awareness of government and personal spending it opens the eyes of the reader to a problem that has gone unspoken.

Born in Guyana, a third world country in Africa, Dr. Jaikara, moved to England as a young adult and spent ten years in medical school and another seven years in America honing his skills as a plastic surgeon, eventually opening his own practice in Humble, Texas a municipality of Houston. Approached by a local bank to join their board of directors he accepted this position. Dr. Jaikara began studying global monetary systems.

That is when he discovered the fatal flaw in the current economic system. Giving the reader knowledge of his background, where he came from and where his authority comes from to be able to write on this matter, he relates to his audience and shows he is very well educated. Reading his background, you are assured after seventeen years of schooling, when he was on the board of directors for a bank, he absorbed all of the information available to him.

The reason he writes this book is that he feels he must share the knowledge he attained, not because he needs fame or wealth. Note that he is a plastic surgeon, but because people must know this in order to save themselves and the world. He predicts that the complete downfall of the economy will be in 2012.

Based on the current rate of debt and inflation, the economy will no longer be able to sustain itself and will fall victim to the fates of previous civilizations such as Egypt, Babylonia, Rome, Persia and Greece. In these civilizations, similar economic structures led to only a small percentage of the population holding all of the wealth. When only a few people hold the wealth, there is no one to buy and no one to sell.

Examination of the Money System

Dr. Jaikara looks at the elementary theories of economics and questions the fundamentals. Take the explanation of inflation; caused by the United States Government creating money to pay for its expenditures. However, if the government or anyone for that matter had the power to create money for their expenditures, would they ever be in debt?

The device creating the all-debt monetary system are the bonds issued by the government. The government prints these bonds, an interest bearing instrument, and uses them as collateral to borrow money from the privately owned banking industry. The Treasury prints the actual dollar bills when the Federal Reserve requests.

The government holds the Treasury, but the Federal Reserve is comprised of privately held corporations. This creates money from thin air for the public expenditure but is it possible to pay the principal of the debt plus interest, where does the additional money for interest come from?

Where We Are

The author asks this insightful question, which may seem simple at first, but once you begin to think about it, it becomes perplexing. Eventually you end up going in circles reflecting on the answer, which is exactly where we stand in our monetary system. If new money is created with interested owed, the interest must come from another's debt to pay another.

This suggests that the economy must continually grow to keep up with the demand. Noting the cycles of the economy, Dr. Jaikara says that these are only the symptoms of a bad monetary system, such as foreclosures, failing businesses and the fall of the stock market.

How We Got There

The current monetary system uses the premise that the rate and amount of new loans must be equal to or greater than the rate and amount of loans people are paying back. Therefore, banks must push their loans to the consumers and to entice consumers in this ever-competing free market, they must artificially lower interest rates.

When people become more hesitant to borrow because of the symptoms of bad economics this leads to an economic downfall that the government can only help by creating more money, artificially stimulating the economy creating a higher inflation rate and decreasing the value of the dollar, which in turn will raise costs. This cycle cannot heal itself with the current monetary system.

The Solution

The author proposes that Congress is legally entitled to order the US Treasury to print US notes. In addition, he proposes that the Treasury should be the only authorized source of money in the United States. He suggests it should answer only to the government, leading to the government bypassing the bonds and The Federal Reserve, creating its own money and not owing any interest.

He states this would eliminate the need for income tax as well, since the government will no longer need citizen's income to pay for its debt. This would cause the supply to grow at a rate consistent with need and leads to "economic liberty". People can then keep the money they make and lower their need to constantly live on credit and borrowed dollars.

Two Dates That Radically Changed the Financial World

From time to time, you find events that alter the course of the world. Two dates that radically changed the financial world were the Creation of the Federal Reserve in **1913** and the U.S. Departure from the Gold Standard in **1971**. Both of these events had far ranging effects that still impact your life and that of the world economy today.

The Creation of the Federal Reserve System

The Federal Reserve System is commonly referred to as simply the Fed. This body functions as the United States' central banking system. As a result of a number of financial panics that rocked the U.S. from the late 1800's through an especially bad panic in 1907, congress enacted the Federal Reserve Act in 1913.

The body that began as simply a central bank organization for the United States gradually evolved into an outfit with vast powers and responsibilities. You saw these become especially evident in the Great Recession and accompanying financial crises of the last several years that began in 2007, fully a hundred years after the serious panic that led to the creation of the Fed in the first place.

The Evolving Powers of the Federal Reserve

The Great Depression first led to the expansion of powers and roles of the Federal Reserve System. From a primary role as central banker to the United States, the organization has evolved to its status today as the overseer of the country's financial system stability, conductor of the country's monetary policy, regulator and supervisor of the banking system and institutions, and provider of critical financial services to the banks, savings and loan companies, foreign banks, and the Federal government.

Perhaps the greatest power that the Fed gained in these intervening decades was the ability to set the official interest rates of the United States, in an effort to boost the economy in down periods and prevent it from overheating in periods of rapid expansion and growth.

The Recently Gained Powers of the Federal Reserve

In the financial crises that started in 2007, the Fed began to flex its muscles in a titanic effort to save the American based economic system and world economies. You saw the broadest definition imaginable for "stabilizing the nation's financial system" interpreted. Suddenly the Fed began accepting questionable and vaguely valued assets of risky real estate, sub prime loans, and even derivatives as collateral from banks in desperate needs of immediate cash transfusions.

More like blood transfusions, these emergency loans totaled up to trillions of dollars. Without them, you have heard that the entire financial system would have collapsed completely and in a matter of days as a crises of confidence swept the entire Western based financial system.

You can easily see how the creation of the Fed proved to be a first date that radically altered the financial world in the last hundred years. There was yet a second date that saw an even more radical shift in the financial world. The American, and subsequently rest of the world, abandonment of the gold standard in 1971 caused earth shattering ramifications in the balance of the global financial system for both the United States and the entire world. You have possibly heard this referred to as the Nixon Shock before.

The Gold Standard

The gold standard and Breton Woods Agreements were the bedrock framework for the world financial system following the economic devastation of World War II. In this system of foreign exchange control, the dollar and other major world foreign currencies such as the British Pound, Swiss Franc, German Deutsche Mark, Canadian Dollar, French Franc, and others, all had direct values to the price of gold. This led to a generally stable international financial regime and economies.

By the time the 1970's arrived, the United States had reached the point that both increasing domestic program spending and the Vietnam War created a simultaneous trade deficit and a deficit in balance of payments. These proved to be the first in the entire twentieth century for America. In the year 1970, the dollar declined in gold coverage from fifty-five percent down to twenty-two percent, representing a staggering decline of thirty-three percentage points.

The Austrian School of Economics, along with the Neoclassical Economists, highlight this year as the point where foreign holders of the American dollar finally lost their belief in the ability of the United States government to cut both trade and budget deficits.

If you were an adult in those tumultuous years, you will remember the economic turbulence that these events caused.

The End of the Gold Standard

You may recall that the next year, 1971, saw the American government print even more dollars to pay the domestic and military spending bills. Washington printed fully ten percent more dollars that they then dispatched overseas. Confidence in the U.S. dollar was quickly crumbling, as $22 billion in physical assets were withdrawn from the United States in only the first six months of the year.

The U.S. was not the first country to abandon the Breton Woods agreement. West Germany made the first leap to avoid the inevitable inflation that they saw coming to the U.S. economy and dollar as a result of the reckless economic behavior that the U.S. had begun practicing.

After this, the other major economies of Western Europe started demanding more gold from the U.S. as fulfillment of its promise to actually pay the bills. The U.S. gold reserves began sinking rapidly, as both Switzerland and France demanded hundreds of millions of dollars in gold.

Switzerland became the second country to leave the Breton Woods agreement. Not to be outdone, and with the dollar tanking against other currencies and gold, President Richard Nixon finally decided to end the U.S. dollar to gold convertibility. In one swift move, he abandoned both the gold standard and the Breton Woods system, which more or less collapsed with the U.S. forsaking honest gold accountability.

The Results of the U.S. Departing from the Gold Standard

The resulting chaos that wracked currencies and financial markets over the next ten plus years demonstrated what a radical decision abandoning gold proved to be. Before Nixon withdrew from the dollar to gold convertibility agreement in 1971, the U.S. dollar stood at between $40 and $44 per ounce of gold. Within a year of Nixon leaving the gold standard in 1972, the dollar had dropped to an average of almost $64 per ounce.

This represented a staggering more than fifty percent drop in the value of the dollar in only that first year. The situation only became worse with time, as the dollar continued to crash and burn. 1973 saw an average gold price of $106.50 per ounce, 1974 witnessed $183 plus average price per ounce, and by 1980 gold had risen to nearly $595 per ounce against the dollar. The other way of saying this is, of course, that the dollar had dropped from only $42 per ounce average in 1971 to $595 per ounce by 1980, representing an unbelievable over 1,300 percent drop in the dollar in less than ten years.

Though the dollar managed to stabilize in the next few decades, with gold fluctuating wildly over the next twenty or so years, the continuing decline of the dollar since Nixon abandoned the gold standard only continues to this day.

2520% Inflation in 40 Years!

For 2009, the average gold price was $972, while the 2010 full year price is set to be over $1,100 per ounce. Since the gold standard and Breton Woods agreement were discarded then, the U.S.

dollar has collapsed from around $42 per ounce to more than $1,100 per ounce. This represents a crushing nearly 2,520% in forty years.

When you wonder how significant an event withdrawing from the gold standard and Breton Woods treaty was, consider this.

The government publishes an inflation rate that averages two to four percent per year. Yet gold tells us that the dollar has actually dropped more than 60% per year on average over the last forty years. Leaving the gold standard caused a radical change in the financial world.

Most likely history will repeat itself and hyperinflation will be the end of this cycle. After that we may finally learn something and create a better system.

Why Banking Is The Most Lucrative Business Model

You may have wondered in the past what the best legal model that exists for making money is. Without any doubt, you can be sure that it is banking.

Although you may be surprised by this answer, the reason that banking is so unbelievably lucrative lies in the concept of the fractional reserve banking system.

The history and practice of this system shows that not only is it wildly profitable and completely legal, but that it is actually encouraged and backed up by the central banks and governments of the world.

History of Fractional Reserve Banking

Fractional reserve banking is a relatively newer concept that only arose within the last three hundred years. Before the 1800's, people who saved their money kept it in silver and gold coins. These early savers needed a secure place to store their precious metal money. This role was filled by the goldsmiths of Europe.

The Goldsmiths' Evolution

In receipt of a given quantity of gold or silver coins, the local gold-smith would issue a note for this form of deposit. Over some time, such notes evolved into a well trusted medium for exchange. You saw the creation of the earliest forms of paper money in these goldsmiths' notes.

The goldsmiths proved to be a shrew bunch. As they watched these notes being used for exchange directly, they noticed that the majority of their customers did not come to cash in their gold and silver notes all at once.

They smelled an opportunity to not only collect fees for storing their customers' deposits of gold and silver bullion, but also to invest these reserves of coins into loans and bills that paid interest. While this did leave the goldsmiths with more notes issued than they had on hand in actual gold and silver reserves to pay them, it also created a nice second stream of income for them.

In this resulting process, the goldsmiths changed from being only storehouses for precious metals who received fees for keeping them safe. Instead, they became interest earning and interest paying banks. You saw the birth of the fractional reserve banking system like this.

The problems with these early banks lay in the matter of confidence. When the holders of this originally deposited gold, their creditors, lost faith for whatever reason in these banks ability to pay back their notes in gold or silver, then a number of the depositors who had become creditors might attempt to cash out their notes all at once.

A bank would be forced to attempt to call in loans or sell bills for gold and silver to pay the depositors their money back. When these banks failed at the task, they either defaulted on their gold and silver notes or went bankrupt. As a result, you saw the rise of the modern day problem of bank runs that led to the ruin of numerous early banking institutions.

The Rise of Central Banks

Because banks were failing at dangerous rates, financial crises began to occur more frequently. Finally, the governments of the major countries and economies of the world had enough. Their answer to the all too common and persistent problem was to create an institution that you are aware of today, the central bank.

These central banks were not always government, or public, institutions. Sometimes they were privately held operations. Whichever form they took, central banks were organizations that had the national authority to regulate and oversee these commercial banks, function as an emergency lender in times of lower liquidity or cash on hand, and create minimum reserve requirements. The creation and subsequent rise of central banks greatly reduced these dangers of the early fractional reserve banking system.

The Idea of The Fractional Reserve Banking Explained

Now that you know the history of the rise of the fractional reserve banking system, it is helpful to understand how this system forms the bedrock of the money supply, as well as the banking profit model, today.

In fractional reserve banking, banks are not only permitted, but encouraged, to maintain only a fraction of their actual deposits in reserve forms of cash and other easily liquidated assets.

The rest becomes check book money, or numbers on a computer screen, that they are then able to loan out and invest. Fractional reserve banking goes a step further. It happens every day as the banks loan out money that they do not have in their vaults rather than only money that has been deposited by their customers. Every modern commercial bank engages in this legalized money creation banking scheme.

In theory, fractional reserve banking is utilized to significantly expand the available money supply, or amount of cash and on demand deposits available, to an amount that it cold not otherwise reach. As a result of this fractional reserve banking system practice, you will find that the overall money supply of the majority of nations proves to be a multiple greater than the literal amount of tangible money that the country's central bank has created.

You may have heard this multiple be referred to as the money multiplier. Regulatory groups create it by fixing the exact reserve requirement as a financial ratio for commercial banks to follow. In the United States, this money multiplier commonly works at a ratio of 20:1. You heard that right, banks are able to loan out twenty times as much money as they have in deposits on hand.

Specific Ways that the Fractional Reserve Banking System Benefits Banks

You have already seen the general ways that the fractional reserve banking system benefits banks. Being able to loan out twenty times as much money as they take in from deposits is an enormous legal advantage. Still, it only benefits them if they can make money on it.

You are no doubt an unknowing participant in their scheme to make enormous profits. If you have a credit card in your wallet, then you are probably paying upwards of twenty percent in interest on any balance that you carry. Mortgages and car loans only bring in from four to ten percent interest for the banks, but this is still an enormous return on money that they are legally able to create out of thin air.

For example, you deposit $1,000 in a bank. The bank gives you a receipt and cheerfully agrees to pay you, the customer, one percent interest per year, or $10 annually. The bank then starts thinking about ways to loan out the now $20,000 that this money multiplier effect creates literally out of thin air.

Assuming that they are able to make a car loan for an eight percent interest rate, then they will realize $1,600 in interest that first year. After paying you the $10 interest payment, they are left with an astonishing $1,590 profit for the year. Their return in this case is a massive one hundred and fifty-nine percent. You will probably agree that this is not a shabby return for simply holding your money and then making a car loan off of it.

You probably are not laughing as you think about the fact that the bank pays you a mere one percent in interest on your deposits that they then use at a ratio of 20:1 in order to bring in from four to twenty percent interest payments.

Even if you are receiving a more generous three to four percent interest on a certificate of deposit, the banks are still laughing long and hard. The joke is how they pay you a mere fraction of the interest that they are legally allowed to garner for themselves on not only your money, but twenty times the money that you entrust to them.

There is not any other business model in existence under the sun that is both legal and allows an entity to generate money on the fly, from thin air. Doing this, the banks make enormous returns in interest, translating to titanic profits, and all of this with practically no work involved. If this were not a government sanctioned practice and establishment, you would no doubt call it a racket.

The New Banking Rules And How They Affect Your Money

Since the financial collapse of several years ago, the world's banking regulators have been attempting to craft a set of rules that would prevent another financial calamity on the scale seen in 2008.

Now in the very month of the two year anniversary of the spectacular and tragic collapse of Lehman Brothers, you have seen them come together to endorse a new group of regulations that will dramatically alter the ways that banks do business in the future.

These new rules will have far ranging repercussions for not only the banking industry, but for you and your access to money as well.

Background of the New Banking Rules

You may remember that it was not that long ago that the financial crisis caused the world's banking system to be hours away from total collapse. Regulators from the U.S. and especially the European Union have been struggling to come together on an agreement for significantly tougher regulation and oversight of the banks since then.

Early September's new agreement that is intended to safeguard the world economic system from ongoing financial crises and to protect the worldwide banking industry achieves far ranging affects that will start to take effect in only a few years and be phased in over the next ten years.

The New Banking Rules

A variety of new rules are coming into effect as a result of the sweeping new regulation agreed on. These new rules begin by increasing the capital reserve ratio that banks have to keep by more than three hundred percent.

Capital reserve ratios are the amount of money that banks are required to keep as a cushion in the event of possible significant losses. Banks will now have to keep a common equity position, the lowest risk form of capital, of seven percent of assets instead of the former two percent of such assets.

This common equity is comprised of profits that are not paid out in dividends, as well as the money that shareholders have put into a company's stock. These conservative forms of assets are what banks must hold against riskier assets going forward. This is known as a leverage ratio.

The higher leverage ratio is an effort to make the banks keep significant reserves for all of the money that they place at risk. It is intended to not let them play games with the accounting rules any longer. The intention is to force banks to take on more conservative investments. Indeed, you should expect to see these new rules majorly impact the ways that banks conduct their business going forward.

As part of this new seven percent common equity position reserve requirement, there will be a two and a half percent buffer amount that banks are allowed to draw on when they are faced with crisis. Restrictions on how much they are able to offer as bonuses and pay to executives, as well as how much money can be distributed out to shareholders will accompany the use of these funds.

Besides these new capital reserves, the Basel Committee on Banking Supervision is also enacting new ways to help banks protect themselves when they get involved in activities that are not banking related. They are similarly enforcing new ways that banks will be able to work with off balance sheet investments.

The goal in these changes is to increase transparency in the financial world. Banks will be offered incentive to engage in the trading of exotic investments and instruments on regulated open markets. This contrasts with the present practice of quiet and secretive trading between the banks. Loopholes would be closed to stop banks from cheating.

It is worth noting that the G-20 meeting will have to approve the final rules before they are completely enacted. Individual countries will have to ratify them as well. These votes are expected to yield positive results for the new rules. The U.S. in particular is behind them and even wanted more aggressive rules under President Obama. Countries will then have until January 1, 2013 to start implementing the rules, which are being called Basel III.

Repercussions of the New Banking Rules

Banks are already sounding alarms about what these new banking rules will mean for them. Profits will be lower, weaker banks will struggle to manage, and the cost of borrowing will be increased.

A number of banking industry groups are out warning about how these newer more conservative capital rules will make them reduce credit offered, leading to economic growth that is crippled.

If you are a borrower, then you will find that your access to credit may be significantly restricted. This is because the significantly higher capital level being required of banks will lessen their available reserves to lend out. This will likely lead to fewer loans being made, less credit being issued, and higher rates being charged for these important services to customers.

Naturally, this is not the intention. The goal is to encourage banks to engage in activities that lead to sustainable growth and stability in the world financial markets. You already hear many experts acknowledge that there will be an increase in the costs of borrowing, though. These people claim that this is a reasonable and acceptable price to pay for a financial system that is less likely to catch on fire and burn completely down. Banks will be able to take a significant hit from a financial pull back without being destroyed.

Banks will not have to begin implementing the rules regarding the higher common equity levels until 2013. They will actually have until 2019 until the more drastic measures take full effect. Still, you will begin to see the effects of tighter credit, higher standards, and more elevated interest rates before this as banks begin to adjust their practices to be in compliance.

Other Impacts of the New Banking Rules

The new higher reserve leverage ratios are going to create other impacts on the major banks as well. Some of the world's major banks do not have the seven percent capital ratio available presently. They will have to begin raising significant amounts of money almost immediately.

Among the banks in this uncomfortable position are several important banks in various members of the developed world. German's Landesbanks is one of them that may have to come up with an additional $63 billion to meet the new regulations for reserves. The country's largest bank, Deutsche Bank, is another that is having to increase reserves. They are selling stock valued at around $13 billion partly to cover the new requirements.

Besides this, France's Societe Generale and Lloyds Bank in Great Britain will have to raise other capital money too. In the United States, the effect is expected to be different. Banks here will also have to ramp up capital amounts, but you may see weaker ones who are not able to do so. These may be required to enter into mergers with stronger banks in order to survive. The net effect of this will be a shrinking number of banks. Fewer banks means less choices for consumers and less competition to keep the banks user friendly for consumers.

U.S. regulators have also hinted that they may enforce harsher rules on some banks. Those that are considered to be systemically important, or critical for the banking system, could be regulated even more strictly. This is because their problems might easily spread from one bank to the next.

Expect Higher Fees With The 2010 Banking Reform

The deregulation of the banking industry began in the late 1970s with states adopting new laws to reform and permit banks to branch within and beyond state lines. It is for this reason that we now see these super banks who are under the false assumption that they are too big to fail.

Scholars today hypothesize that the need for banking reform is predicated on two motives of the federal government: to intervene and correct a failing market and to increase competition for the benefit of boosting national morale and enhancing the quality of life of its citizenry.

This new banking reform for you means that banks must develop better risk management plans so that you as the consumer do not have to pay for future bank failures; and this also means that you can expect to pay lower interest rates on some banking products.

Banking Regulation: History in Perspective

According to Randall Kroszner, a professor of economics who teaches at the Graduate School of Business at the University of Chicago, scholars hypothesize that the reason for the current banking reform rests on the public interest theory.

The theory holds that the government is motivated to only intervene in state affairs when the market suffers significant failure to the point that competition decreases, creating a loss in state revenues.

In his article entitled, The Motivations Behind Banking Reform, Kroszner discusses how state legislatures began to seek additional revenues as sources of income to offset future and potential losses associated with laws that prohibited states from issuing money and imposing a state tax for interstate commerce.

As an effective solution, states began to charter banks and impose fees. To further generate revenue income, they owned a controlling interest in the bank by buying shares and they also levied taxes against the bank. This created a great opportunity for state legislatures.

Since they couldn't receive charter fees from out-of-state branches, the legislature of one state began to restrict banks from operating within certain regions. Their purpose was to restrict competition by prohibiting interstate and local bank branching operations. These actions contributed to the creation of monopolies in which the state prevented banks from building branches within a particular city to both restrict and monitor competition. All the while they continued to charge fees.

The 2010 Implications of Banking Reform

On June 25, 2010, congressional and senate leaders etched out a bill to change banking practices. The new legislation creates the following key opportunities that will benefit you as the consumer.

The new legislation creates a consumer protection agency. It restricts banks from dubious trading practices. It limits risk management practices in relation to banking acquisitions and operations.

Consumer Protection: The new agency will be a part of the Federal Reserve system. This means that there will be a greater protection of your assets. With the Federal Reserve as the main support system, you can rest assured that legislation will curb excessive mortgage and lending practices. For you, there won't be extra and unnecessary charges of overdraft fees.

Trading Credit Default Swaps: The Federal Reserve now requires that banks change how they do business with credit default swaps (CDS). A credit default swap is a credit derivative. It is a bilateral contract in which there is a protection buyer and a protection seller. With a CDS, the protection buyer makes payments to the protection seller. The CDS may be a loan or bond obligation of a corporation or a government entity, who is called the reference entity (reference obligor).

In the event that the corporation or a government entity defaults, the protection buyer will make a one-time payment to the protection seller before the contract is subsequently terminated. This financial instrument is very risky because it is not insurance. Each party to the contract assumes a risk, the protection buyer suffering the greatest risk because the protection seller doesn't have to be a regulated entity and is not required by law to maintain a reserve system.

What does this mean for you as the consumer?

Before the reform, banks could make risky investments with un-regulated entities, which meant that your money or your assets could be used to pay off protection buyers in the event of a default. This makes sense because banks typically traded credit default swaps between themselves.

Today, because of the reform, instead of banks trading these in-struments without some form of monitoring and regulation policy, they must now include a third-party. The presence of a third-party makes the financial transactions that are typically complex more transparent for you and other entities.

Risk Management Reform:

Banks typically develop policies to manage risk. In the case of the recent bailouts, risk management planning failed to secure banks from insolvency. Therefore, with the new banking reform legisla-tion, the Federal Reserve has the power to liquidate a bank's assets. This will ensure that you, as the taxpayer, will not have to pay for future bailouts.

Taxpayers should not be responsible for failing banks. You should not have to pay for banks that have failed to secure your money. You should not have to pay for corporate greed and the banks should not be able to receive tax a benefit. If a bank fails to man-age their risks, then that bank should seek other suitable measures. This is the purpose of developing a sound risk management policy.

Global Implications and International Banking Reform

Other country leaders are beginning to coordinate their efforts at establishing better banking regulations. As they study the United States legislative activities and reform policies, foreign countries are beginning to consider changing their own laws and policies in favor of a more global financial system.

This is the sentiment of the International Monetary Fund. Dominique Strauss Kahn, the head of the agency, stressed the need for global change in terms of financial reform. He states, "My concern is that even if it's right when you look from the country side - what the US is doing, what the European Union wants to do, what the Japanese wants to do - there may be some inconsistency when you look at all this together. That's why we're trying to push for is a more coordinated, more global way to answer this question, and to put in place a new kind of regulation" (Public Radio International, Matthew Bell).

The IMF (International Monetary Fund) stresses the need for a global banking tax. This is great for the U.S. consumer. To know exactly what you will be charged on a particular item or financial instrument would be an ideal situation. When you visit these countries, there are no clear rules about taxes charged to certain items. This makes it easier for not only the foreign banks, but also the U.S. banks that operate in foreign countries to charge excessive fees to the consumer unlearned in credit derivatives and complex financial transactions regulation.

Banking Reform Costs to the Consumer

Now that we know that banking reform is here to stay, here are a few benefits and costs to remember.

Bank Rates: You can expect to pay a lower interest rate for a certificate of deposit.

Checking Account: You can expect to pay a higher checking account fee. Since banks are being criticized for their overdraft fee structures, they will go back to the old-fashioned way of charging fees. That means you might have to come up with ten to fifteen dollars a month for your checking account.

Balance Minimum: Banks typically allow you the benefit of keeping your monthly fee as long as you have the lowest balance minimum in your account. This is typically a range of $300 to $2,000, depending on the type of account. With the new banking reform, expect to deposit more in your accounts in order to keep the monthly maintenance fee all to yourself.

Sources:

- The Motivations Behind Banking Reform by Randall Kroszner

- Public Radio International: Global implications of US banking reform by Matthew Bell

- Banking Reform and You: What Will It Cost? (Part 2 of 3) by Richard Barrington

<u>HISTORY</u>

"Events That Shaped Our Present"

Money From Thin Air - The Fractional Banking System

The Origins of Fractional Banking

The fundamental idea governing the fractional banking system dates back to medieval England. Between 1000 and 1100 A.D., money lenders, who were at that time referred to as goldsmiths, secured the people's gold and silver in their vaults. With each deposit of gold or silver, the depositors were given a paper receipt designating the amount that they had entrusted to the goldsmiths.

These receipts began to acquire a value of their own and function as the currency of choice, as the people, quite naturally, preferred the convenience of carrying paper receipts rather than hauling around cumbersome sacks of gold and silver. Aware of this and the fact that the depositors rarely returned to the vaults to withdraw the full value of their deposits, the goldsmiths started to loan the receipts out to customers and charge interest on them.

As long as they had sufficient reserves in the vault to satisfy the withdrawal demands of their customers, they could profit on the interest earned from their loans. The issuance of these loans, however, was not backed by silver and gold that the goldsmiths actually had inside their vaults.

Given the improbability that all the depositors would at one time come to withdraw their savings, the goldsmiths essentially inaugurated the system of fractional banking, whereby they maintained only a fraction of the total amount of the money that they had actually loaned out. Simply put, because the paper receipts were seen as legitimate currency, they were able to loan out money that didn't exist in the hope that there wouldn't be a run on the bank.

Highlights in the Historical Development of Modern-Day Fractional Banking

Once this idea gained momentum and was accepted as a viable form of money circulation, a long power struggle ensued between bankers and government officials.

A man by the name of Amshall Moses Bower, perhaps better known by his businesses moniker, Rothschild, was responsible for bringing the benefits of fractional banking to bear upon governments and kings as opposed to simply restricting it to individual investors.

The Bank of England was also very much a creation inspired by the same ambitions motivating the Rothschilds. Far more money was able to be made when the tax revenue of an entire country was used as collateral and the interest accrued from the issuance of huge loans greatly enhanced the bankers power to loan out prodigious sums of money.

Before the American Revolutionary War in 1776, the colonies had been printing their own money and using it in a way that reflected the true nature of the laws of supply and demand.

When King George III began worrying about paying back England's mounting debt to the bankers as a result of the wars England had been engaged in, he was forced to exact a heavy taxation on the colonies and to prohibit the use of Colonial Script, the legal tender being used in the American colonies. Benjamin Franklin attributed the war's primary cause to this event.

President Abraham Lincoln demonstrated his disapproval of the system when he started having "green backs" printed to finance the Civil War. Most of the powerful financial institutions in Europe were threatened by the prospect of a united America and therefore wielded their power in influencing the way the war would be financed.

Lincoln was faced with prohibitive interest rates when he went to New York in an effort to secure loans for the war effort. It was after his rejection of the terms, that he went on to print the greenbacks with the approval of the Congress. Seeing the success of the American government's own issuance of legal tender, the European bankers harshly chastised Lincoln's system in the media, resulting in the eventual creation of the National Bank Act which forced the government to offer bonds to the banks so that they could in turn use them to secure bank notes.

The government bonds backed the bank notes. In other words, it was a way to impose the fractional banking system on America and give commanding power to the national banks. Lincoln had resolved to repeal the National Bank Act and return the economy back to one based on the government's issuance of money but was assassinated shortly after his re-election.

How the Federal Reserve Controls Money

Following Lincoln's death the struggle for who would control the flow of money, the government or the bankers, waged on. It wasn't until 1913, when the Federal Reserve Act was created that the system we have today was firmly set in place.

Essentially, the act put the power of money creation into the hands of the Federal Reserve. Their primary function is to loan money out to private banks, whereby they can control the circulation of money and the rate of inflation. When they want to expand the economy, they set low interest rates in order that more loans can be secured.

The reverse happens when they wish to slow the economy down, namely, through the raising of interest rates. This whole process is built on the Fed's purchasing or selling of U.S. securities on the open market. To pump more money into the economy, the Fed buys the interest earning securities from the public and in contrast, sells them when they wish to contract the market economy.

The more money in circulation translates into lower interest rates and vice versa. The Fed also sets the fractional reserve levels for the banks and uses this power to further control the supply of money. This system is played out on a global scale through the central banks control of monetary policy in a majority of other countries.

How Today's Fractional Banking System Works

The basic premise of the current fractional banking system, namely the creation of phantom money, is relatively the same as the one used by the goldsmiths in medieval England.

To illustrate, a person deposits $100 into bank A. The reserve requirement for banks is 10%. This in turn means that the bank is required to keep on hand at least $10 of the $100 that the person deposited. The other $90 can be used by the bank to offer loans or to enter into other investments. If the bank decides to loan that money out, then the loan recipient will of course be charged interest.

Now, let's say the loan recipient writes a check of $90 using the loan money, that money will then be deposited into another bank, bank B, by whoever received the check.

Bank B is entitled to loan out $81 or 10% of that $90 deposited. As this process continues, the original $100 will have ultimately created $1000 in money. Imagining this taking place on a much larger monetary scale and on a daily basis, one can see how the fractional banking system has served to create an entirely virtual reality of financial transactions.

Banking Institutions Are Dangerous To Our Liberties

Thomas Jefferson was born into a prominent and wealthy Virginia family on April 13, 1743. He was a Renaissance man who spent his entire life championing the independence of a country and its people.

Jefferson strongly opposed the "artificial aristocracy founded on wealth and birth, without either virtue or talents" and, instead, fought for state's rights, limited federal government, and the people's right to govern themselves. His strong views on the banking system can be summarized by the quote:

"I believe that banking institutions are more dangerous to our liberties than standing armies. If the American people ever allow private banks to control the issue of their currency, first by inflation, then by deflation, the banks and corporations that will grow up around the banks will deprive the people of all property - until their children wake up homeless on the continent their fathers conquered. The issuing power should be taken from the banks and restored to the people where it properly belongs."

- Thomas Jefferson, 1802

Youngest Lawyer to Practice Law

At the age of twenty-three, Jefferson became the youngest lawyer to practice law before Virginia's highest court and only one year later, he began serving in Virginia's House of Burgesses, a legislative body similar to the British Parliament. With the British passage of the Coercive Acts of 1774, in response to the Boston Tea Party, Jefferson wrote a concise and moving set of resolutions called: "A Summary View of the Rights of British America".

The pamphlet garnered the young man considerable respect as a writer, philosopher and future statesman. The summary eloquently presented arguments for why the new nation had the right, and should seek, to self-govern. Among those reasons was Jefferson's argument that America was conquered, and her settlements made, and firmly established, at the expense of individuals, and not of the British public.

Their own blood was spilt in acquiring lands for their settlement, their own fortunes expended in making that settlement effectual; for themselves they fought, for themselves they conquered, and for themselves alone they have right to hold.

Not a shilling was ever issued from the public treasures of his majesty, or his ancestors, for their assistance, till of very late times, after the colonies had become established on a firm and permanent footing. These resolutions were a precursor to the enormous contribution Jefferson and his writing abilities would play as a founding father on the political stage of a young, struggling nation.

The Second Continental Congress

At the age of 32, following the outbreak of the American Revolutionary War in June of 1775, Jefferson began serving as a delegate from Virginia to the Second Continental Congress. Congress was preparing to draft both a resolution and a declaration of independence seeking to outline their right to independence as well as build the framework from which the new nation would be governed. As one of five men appointed to a committee to draft a declaration Jefferson was tasked with writing the first draft.

The committee made few changes to Jefferson's draft and it was quickly presented to Congress on June 28, 1776. Once the resolution of independence was approved, Congress turned their attention to the committee declaration draft. On July 4, 1776, the Second Continental Congress approved the offical version of the Declaration of Independence. It was to become one of the most important documents in the history of the United States Of America.

The Secretary of State

One year before Jefferson was appointed Secretary of State, President George Washington appointed Alexander Hamilton, Secretary of Treasury. The two men had radically opposing viewpoints on the type of fiscal policy that should govern national banking and currency. Jefferson, a Southern man, envisioned a nation of agriculture and personal freedoms where as Hamilton favored manufacturing and industrialization similar to Europe.

Hamiliton was a proponent of the Central Banking system and set out to convince Congress to charter a privately owned company to mint and circulate currency. At the time, the country had accumulated a significant war debt of approximately $42,000.

Hamilton believed these debts should be spread equally among the states while Jefferson, believing strongly in states rights and independence, wanted each state to be held responsible for only the debt they had incurred.

Hamilton continued to push President Washington for the Central Banking system that would be given the responsibility of handling payment of the debts as well as receive deposits of government funds, tax revenue, and supply the country with currency needed for growth.

The Bank of the United States would be financed with $10 million dollars, 80% of which would be owned by private stock holders while the remaining 20% would be retained by the United States government. Stock holders could be domestic or foreign though foreign shareholders would not be given voting rights.

Of the 25 member Board of Directors, 20 were to be elected by the stockholders and only 5 would be government appointed. Jefferson lost the argument and the Bank of the United States was established. Jefferson resigned at Secretary of State in 1793 but remained heavily entrenched in politics until his presidency.

The Presidency

After serving four years as Vice President, Jefferson won a fierce battle for Presidency against Aaron Burr. Jefferson's intent as President was to instill the morals and beliefs of the Democratic-Republican Party he had helped to create but he required the help of Alexander Hamilton to break the deadlock in the House of Representatives. Jefferson was forced to make difficult concessions including leaving the national banking and tariff programs, created under Hamilton, in force.

While much of Jefferson's presidency was focused on reducing the federal government and cutting the national debt, the events of 1802 at the port of New Orleans changed things. Under French control, New Orleans was closed to U.S. commercial trade, the very thing Jefferson had relied on for national funding.

When Jefferson realized the potential hazard to the economy, he began negotiations with Napolean about the purchase of Louisiana. With little opposition from Congress the purchase was completed in 1803, effectively doubling the size of the United States for the cost of approximately $15 million dollars. Though domestically unpopular at the time, it became one of Jefferson's crowning achievements as the third President of the United States.

The Presidency was the last major political office Jefferson held before retiring to Monticello. This was the home he had spent years building on the land he inherited from his father. Most of Jefferson's 83 years of life were spent quietly but effectively advocating for personal liberties in a deliberate, thoughtful manner.

The story of his life stands as a remarkable success story, though it is rarely mentioned that six of his children preceded him in death as well as his wife. As a founding father of a remarkable new nation, Thomas Jefferson was specific that upon his death there were to be only two accomplishments on his tombstone to represent his legacy; the author of the Declaration of Independence and the founder of the University of Virginia.

Thomas Jefferson died, 50 years to the day after the United States Declaration of Independence had been signed, on July 4, 1826.

Money Evolution - From Barter to International Monetary Unit

If you are a student of history, then you know how far that money has come from its origins to the present.

Money has continuously evolved from the earliest forms of barter to fiat money used around the world today.

In the process it has gone through the stages of commodity money, coinage money, trade bills, backed bank bills, and finally to fiat paper money. Each of these had their day in the sun, along with upsides and downsides.

How It All Started - Barter Forms of Money

You may be surprised to learn that the earliest forms of money were not at all money as we think about it today. Hunting and gathering societies before the rise of the first states and empires provided for themselves on a family basis. When they needed something that they did not have or could not obtain personally, they either traded for it or simply gave it away in consideration of future anticipated gifts.

This led to a simpler and more sharing society. The problem with it lay in the fact that you did not have an acceptable medium of exchange to which the buyer and seller could convert the items that they had to trade.

Furthermore, you did not have a standard of value against which a rabbit, deer, or portion of grain or fruits could be measured.

The Rise of Commodity Money

Along with the rise of the first great early civilizations such as the Sumerians in Mesopotamia, which is in modern day Iraq, bigger scale economies began to develop. The Babylonians and their neighbors actually created the first economic systems that you would recognize today. They came up with standard measurements of value, legal contracts, rules concerning debts, and law codes that pertained to private property, trade, and business.

The Law Code of Hammurabi is the first completely preserved law code dealing with exchange and business that we have, dating from almost thirty-eight hundred years ago. In such law codes, the values of commodities such as copper, silver, and bronze were standardized by weight beginning almost five thousand years ago.

Commodity money came into use with these expanding economies and trade. A great number of cultures throughout the world utilized some form of commodity money. In Ancient Africa and China, cowrie shells were used. Japan's medieval feudal system used koku, a warrior's portion of rice for a year. The ancient empires of the Middle East used shekels for weight and currency.

Weight quantities of metal made better forms of money. These earliest forms of currency were imperishable and could be measured, stored, and transported. Their problem lay in the bulky nature of such metals and other stores of value that had to be weighed any time a transaction was affected. When larger transactions took place, this could be a time consuming and onerous task.

As trade and economies increased, a better unit of currency was needed than these measured out commodities.

Standardized Coinage as Money

The first form of money that you would still recognize came about as a result. Coins made from valuable metals like electrum, bronze, gold, and silver were minted for the first known time around twenty-seven hundred years ago. These forms of money were useful and easily recognizable. Their value was standardized. Coins were first minted on a large scale in Lydia, which is in modern day Turkey.

Their common use spread from there throughout the Ionian islands on to the mainland of Greece and beyond around twenty-five hundred years ago. Coins that came to be made from increasingly more valuable precious metals as gold and silver were more easily transportable and stored than bulkier commodities. Since they were standardized, larger transactions could be more effectively carried out.

As a real revolution in the evolution of money, the use of coins lasted throughout the ancient empires of Persia, the Greek and Macedonian empire and kingdoms, through the Roman Empire and into the Middle Ages. Once again though, you saw economic activity outgrow the usefulness of these forms of money, and the time came for another evolution in money.

The Early Form of Promise - Trade Bills

As trade began to rapidly expand around Europe at the tail end of the middle ages around five to seven hundred years ago, a more convenient form of money than coins became necessary. The bustling Italian city states' trade in wine, cloth, wool, tin, silk, and other goods desperately needed credit to grow and expand.

Goods began to be offered to a purchaser for a bill of exchange. This bill of exchange represented the purchaser's promise to pay the seller on a certain date. A seller would be able to take this bill to a merchant banker in advance of the due date and cash it in for a discounted amount before hand.

As the practice grew, such bills began to be utilized as a method of payment by the sellers to buy other goods from their suppliers. In such a way, this earliest form of paper money as credit turned into an exchange medium, as well as a storage of value medium. In the last years of the 1700's and early 1800's in imperial England, you saw such bills of exchange expand to become a critical source of money and credit.

Their downside lay in the inflexibility of trade bill denomination. How did one make change for a trade bill? It required a complicated system of accounting to keep all of the math straight.

The Invention on Paper Money - Bank Notes

Trade continued to expand, and the need for larger amounts of money again pushed another evolution in the form of money used. Commercial banks arose and filled the need by issuing the first paper money. This money could be redeemed for a set amount of gold or silver coins on demand. In this way, bank notes were a modern day form of representative money.

The governments of the great expanding mercantile nations like Great Britain, the United States, and France gradually took over the issuing of bank notes by and in the 1800's. Until this point though, as many as five thousand different institution's bank notes were circulating around the United States alone.

The upsides to paper money were many. As the sizes of transactions grew exponentially, it no longer made sense to carry around heavy coins and confusing bills of trade. Standardized denominations allowed for easy exchange of such bank notes. Still, the many different kinds of notes issued led to confusion and risk. In theory, the number of bank notes that could be issued were also based on available gold and silver reserves held in vaults. This held back the abilities of the booming world economy to expand.

The Final State - Fiat Currencies

The final stage in the evolution of money came in only the last fifty years or so. Fiat money is money that is not backed up by any physical asset or commodity. As the nations of the world began to need greater amounts of money, there simply was not enough gold and silver to back it all up.

Finally, countries like Great Britain and the United States abandoned their historical ties to such precious metals underlying the currencies. The U.S. became the first to completely go to a straight fiat currency in 1971, leading the rest of the world to make the leap to Fiat Paper money as well.

Money value now came from the promise of the government to honor and back up paper money instead. Now money could be created as needed to keep up with economic activity and expansion.

The evolution of money from a tangible source and store of value to one based on only faith and trust in modern day governments had been completed.

This stage of money is also not without controversy, though. Governments are now able to abuse their power to create as much money as they want at will. Since there is no overseeing power, they can print it without limit, leading to high degrees of inflation, or even to hyperinflation.

Future Evolution of Money - the International Monetary Unit

Because of these problems and limitations with fiat currencies that allow individual governments to run wild, another evolution is already in the works in money. You have already heard talk about a truly international monetary unit that will replace the dollar in the possibly near future.

This will be based on either many currencies, or more probably on a single currency issued by the International Monetary Fund or World Bank. This final evolution will make commerce and trade across national boundaries even easier, and help to keep the paper money more honest.

MONEY

"Understanding the Medium of Exchange"

Money

How to Build a Foundation For Your Financial Future

In his book "Rich Dad's Rich Dad's Conspiracy of the Rich: The 8 New Rules of Money," Robert Kiyosaki lays the foundation for the average person to take control of their financial future. Below are the 8 rules as laid out by Robert Kiyosaki.

Rule #1 - Money is Knowledge

You don't have to start out with a lot of money to make a lot of money - what you need is to educate yourself about money and then figure out a strategy that works for you. You are not going to turn your savings into a fortune by taking everything you have and piling it into a couple of stock recommendations you got after watching Jim Cramer or any number of other financial experts you see on television or read on Web site that guarantees you that its stock picks will make you a fortune. Take the time to do the research and figure out a strategy that will work for you.

Rule #2 - Learn How to use Debt

Good debt will generate income, while bad debt only costs you. Taking on a mortgage to pay for your home is an example of bad debt, but that's not to say that you shouldn't use it to purchase a home, which is a necessity.

Good debt puts money in your pocket. An example of good debt is acquiring a house which you plan to rent. You then use that rental money as leverage to pay for the rental property and also to help pay down your mortgage and other expenses.

Rule #3 - Learn How to Control Cash Flow

The CashFlow Quadrant explains that there are four different types of people: employees, specialists, entrepreneurs, and investors. The majority of us, employees and specialists, are being taxed the most, while entrepreneurs and investors are being taxed the least as a result of taking the most risk to help keep the economy moving in a positive direction.

Entrepreneurs and investors typically earn passive income, which flows in on a regular basis with little-to-no effort. Passive income can be generated by rental property, dividends, or profits from a business that you establish. So, in an effort to keep more of our hard-earned money, we need to shift our focus from being employees and specialists to being entrepreneurs and investors.

Rule #4 - Prepare for the Bad Times and You Will Only Know Good Times

With the exception of a few hiccups, the United States has been in a boom cycle for the last 30 years, which means that both the Baby Boomer generation and their children really have no idea what it's like to live through an actual, extended depression.

Kiyosaki suggests: shifting your position in the CashFlow Quadrant from an employee or a specialists to an entrepreneur or investor (ie, Rule #3), invest for cash flow as opposed to capital gains, and investing for inflation.

While this may mean you are not generating a maximum income, these will help shield you from some effects of a recession.

Rule #5 - The Need for Speed

The goal is to make more money than the banks are printing it. Essentially, we need to find ways to maximize our returns over the course of our day. You do this when you take on good debt. Over the course of time you can use the cash flow you are now generating from what was once good debt and is now a profitable venture to generate more good debt, and so on.

This compounding of money will eventually lead to an extremely high cash flow that will help you prepare for the bad times in Rule #4. You could also think of this as reinvesting dividends in a stable company.

Rule #6 - Learn the Language of Money

You need to learn what the common terms and phrases you see on television and read in newspapers, magazines, and on Web sites means. Any attempt to build your wealth without understanding these terms is gambling.

Rule #7 - Life is a Team Sport. Choose Your Team Carefully

Whether you are getting your personal finances on track or your business finances on track, you need to surround yourself with reliable, smart people. If you are running a small business, you would want to surround yourself with good lawyers, accountants, marketing people, and so on.

This will help you build a house of stone that won't fall down that won't wall down at the first sign of trouble, as opposed to a house of cards.

Rule #8 - Since Money is Becoming Worth Less, Learn to Print Your Own

The Federal Reserve is printing money at a blistering pace, and the only way to fight either inflation or deflation is to set it up so that you have a constant stream of money flowing into your pocket. There are four ways to keep money coming in as opposed to going out: start a business; invest in real estate; invest in stocks, bonds, or mutual funds; and invest in commodities. Money tied up in these assets will not be taxed as highly as would traditional earnings.

Why The Value of FIAT Money Will Always Go to Zero

Paper money today is fiat money. Since 1971, real assets have not backed the dollars that Americans spend. Paper dollars have value by government. The government has declared that these printed dollars are legal money.

Because of America's strong economic history, the dollar continues to have perceived value in America and across the globe. Yet that strong history is becoming more distant both in time an in reality. For many reasons, fiat dollars become worth less and less and, by the time people realize this, it may be too late to do anything about it.

A Brief History of Fiat Money

The official money in ancient Rome was the denarius. In 50 AD the denarius was a pure silver coin, the emperors gradually reduced the silver content until the denarius contained less than 0.05% silver. When Rome collapsed, the denarius was unacceptable in exchange for goods and services. China used worthless paper as currency around the 11th century AD.

The currency held value while China expanded its empire, population, and trade surplus. When these slowed, the currency supply continued to increase, which quickly destroyed the economy and the peace.

In France, one attempt at issuing coin-backed paper ended after excessive increases to the money supply and the people could not exchange their now worthless paper notes for coins. In a more recent attempt, the inflated paper franc lost 99% of its value in 12 years. The post WWI Weimar Germany Republic was burdened with severe reparations from its part in WWI. It printed increasingly worthless paper money to pay its debt.

Why Fiat Money Always Decreases to Zero Value

No government has ever been able to discipline its monetary policy. History has shown that fiat currency makes it easier for any government to:

- Do I always feel as though I am behind in my work?
- Do I want myself and my team to be more productive?
- Do I need to find a balance between work and home?
- Do my team members shirk from responsibility?
- Do I struggle with distractions?
- Do I work for a business with frequent turnaround of employees?

Some reasons (called emergencies but are really excuses) for these dangerous economic decisions are:

- The European countries involved in WWII were heavily in debt to the US.
- The US economy was very strong and the value of dollar had appreciated.

- Of all the major world currencies, only the US dollar was backed by gold.
- The US agreed to link the dollar to the gold price of $35 per ounce and exchange gold bullion for dollars.

Some of the consequences of undisciplined government actions with fiat money have been:

- Inflation remains low. Its rise will lower purchasing power and trouble businesses and consumers.
- Interest rates remain low. Its rise will produce many new economic problems.
- Debt and deficit spending are projected to remain very high. Paper fiat money will be worth less and less.
- The dollar has strengthened along with the recent rise in the gold price as Euros are being converted into both dollars and gold. Is this temporary or artificial? Will the dollar fall in value?
- Disruptive terror attacks loom. God forbid that a serious attack is successful.
- Nuclear aspirations of Iran and North Korea are troubling.
- The Middle East seems closer to war than to peace.

America's Move to Fiat Money

Until the great depression, America was on the gold standard and dollar notes could be exchanged for gold. In 1933, the dollar was devalued, but was still backed by gold. With this gold backing along and a strong economy, the US dollar was accepted as the world's reserve currency after WWII.

The economies of most of the countries involved in WWII were in shambles. However, the deficit spending during the Vietnam War caused nations to redeem their weakened dollars. With the increasing depletion of America's gold supply, President Nixon ended the dollar's gold support in 1971.

President Nixon's action turned the US dollar into fiat money that is itself worth nothing and is not backed by assets of real value. At the same time, all of the world currencies that had been pegged to the US dollar since 1945 also became fiat money.

Nevertheless, in 2010, because the US economy had remained relatively strong, the dollar continues to be the world's main reserve currency. Global commodities such as oil and gold are priced in US dollars. While the euro had been strengthening to become an alternative reserve currency, recent trouble in several European economies caused many to sell euros and buy US dollars along with gold and other real assets. The situation in Europe has stabilized for the moment and the euro is currently rising again.

The Growing Weakness of the US Economy

Yet, the dollar's key position in the global economy is increasingly called into question. There are good reasons to question the dollar's value and strength. The US government is guilty of every action that makes fiat money worthless, and the US economy has experienced nearly all the consequences listed above. Current policy is only increasing these effects and putting the US economy at greater risk. Some current and very serious dangers facing the US economy are:

- Do I always feel as though I am behind in my work?
- Do I want myself and my team to be more productive?
- Do I need to find a balance between work and home?
- Do my team members shirk from responsibility?
- Do I struggle with distractions?
- Do I work for a business with frequent turnaround of employees?

These risks could spiral down together and drastically worsen. In addition, other dangers that may face the US economy are:

- The European countries involved in WWII were heavily in debt to the US.
- The US economy was very strong and the value of dollar had appreciated.
- Of all the major world currencies, only the US dollar was backed by gold.
- The US agreed to link the dollar to the gold price of $35 per ounce and exchange gold bullion for dollars.

Greece nearly defaulted on its obligations, a situation that had all of Europe scrambling. Fears that its default could topple the precarious economies of Portugal, Spain, and Ireland spurred the world to loan Greece money and give it time to correct its problems.

How much time? More debt for Greece is an additional long-term burden. Will it be able to fix its problems in the midst of violent unrest? What about other countries on the brink of disaster? Which may (almost) default next?

If theses smaller economies fall, the larger economies of France, England, and Germany will be at grave risk as well.

Global Impact if the Fiat Dollar Becomes Worthless

World economies are connected and many will fall if the US dollar becomes worthless. Countries holding US dollar in reserve will be weakened. Even if some creditor nations with vibrant economies are able to maintain value in their currency, the impact of the dollar's crash will be severe.

The world needs America to be strong and buy its products. For example, China may be able to withstand the loss of its US dollars and debt, but if America cannot afford to buy its goods, at best a large number of Chinese factories and businesses will close.

Whether the fall of the US dollar precipitates worldwide economic collapse, or the collapse begins elsewhere in the world does not matter. Many national economies are on the verge of default or collapse and could quickly tumble. Yet, in the face of these concerns, governments still seem to be lending and spending, increasing debt and deficits, the very actions that have brought the globe to the edge of the precipice.

Follow These 3 Actions To Lower Your Financial Burden

If you are a member of the middle class, then you will probably agree that the financial crises of the last several years has been absolutely devastating.

Between the free fall plunging of the value of your home, the elimination or at least severe reduction of your credit cards and available lines of credit, the steep decline in the value of your retirement accounts, and the possible loss of your job, you, along with the rest of the middle class, have suffered terribly.

The good news is that you can engage in several practical actions today in order to lower your financial burden.

Lower the Cost of Your Residence Monthly Expenses

Somewhere around a third of your monthly budget likely goes into the costs associated with your house or apartment. Since it is one of the biggest, if not the biggest, of your monthly outlays, this is naturally the first place that you should look to cut costs and save some money in these difficult days. There are several different ways that this can be accomplished, depending on whether you rent or own.

Reduce the Costs For Your Rent

If you currently rent an apartment, townhouse, or house, then you should seriously consider discussing the amount of your monthly rent payment with your landlord. This is particularly the case if you have seen your hours at work reduced, have been the victim of a job furlough, or even have lost your job entirely and are presently looking for a new one.

In this economic climate that you find yourself, landlords tend to be more understanding than they were a few years ago. Most of them would rather knock a few hundred dollars a month off of the rent than see you have to break lease and move out. The only protection that they have in this event is to seize your deposit, which they will likely do should you decide to move out before the lease is up.

You will find yourself in a stronger bargaining position if your lease is about to be up, and it is time for renewal. In the past, this has been the point where the apartment management or owner of the townhouse or house that you rent looked to increase your monthly rent a little bit, under a so called cost of inflation increase.

These days, you will find that many apartment managements and owners are instead willing to lower the monthly price in order to keep you occupying the apartment, townhouse, or house. At least if the landlord is not willing to work with you on lowering the payments, and it is time to renew the lease or move out, then you can move out and recover your deposit monies that you paid.

Once again, in this economic environment, negotiating a new apartment lease or house rental price will be easier than it has been in decades. Today and probably for some time to come, you as a renter will benefit from this new renters' market.

Reduce the Costs For Your Home

If you own your home, then there are two ways that you can potentially lower your monthly housing costs. The quickest and easiest thing that you can do is probably to talk with the bank that holds your mortgage. Tell them that you are in dire financial straits and need to negotiate a lower monthly payment on your mortgage.

The model for this idea comes from the Federal Government's program to adjust mortgages into ones that the mortgage holders can actually afford to pay. Once again, banks are more understanding given the present economic situation than they have been in a long, long time. They will not hang up the phone on you. At the very least, they will hear you out. Even if they say no, it has not cost you anything to try this method of lowering your monthly expenses.

The more traditional means of getting the monthly mortgage payment on your house reduced lies in refinancing your home. You can do this through a variety of sources. You might start out by going down to see the loan officer at your own bank that currently holds your mortgage, in order to talk with them about the lower interest rates that are available these days.

If they are not willing to work with you on a refinance into a more competitive interest rate and monthly mortgage payment, then maybe one of the competing banks will be. You can refinance your mortgage through other ways too. These include going to finance companies, such as ditech.com and greenlightloans.com.

Lower the Cost of Your Television Entertainment Monthly Expense

Although this may come as a surprise, you are probably burning a significant amount of money every month through your television entertainment. Cable and satellite television packages are a luxury that you have likely taken for granted when times were good. Now that the financial crises has forced you to cut back on monthly expenses, this is one area that can be easily trimmed.

Many individuals pay anywhere from $80 to $100 or even more per month for cable or satellite services. You do not have to give up your TV entertainment entirely. By switching over to a Netflix membership, you will be able to have new release quality movie entertainment provided to you in the mail, or over your computer or laptop, for around a dollar per day. By simply doing this, you can save $50 to $80 per month in just that entertainment switch.

Sell Your Luxury Items

Most of you have a variety of items that you do not really need to keep. Included in this category would be boats, jet skis, motorcycles, ATV's, furs, and extra jewelry. Besides providing you with much needed money when you sell them, some of them will reduce your monthly expenses too. Those boats often have to be stored at a marina, and this can prove to be a black hole in your finances.

You have probably heard the expression that a boat is a hole in the water into which you pour money. Gas for boats, as well as for jet skis, motorcycles, and ATV's, adds up quickly, especially at today's still high prices at the pump.

While you may not consider these things to all be luxury items, you should remember that a luxury item is anything that you do not require to support a decent lifestyle, or more simply put, luxuries are things that you can easily do without.

Most Important - Change Your Financial Mindset

You may have not yet come to grips with the fact that things have changed in the United States and its once indomitable economy. Countless jobs have been lost. Many of the prominent economists, like Nouriel Roubini, are saying that these will not ever come back. My personal opinion is that as long as we hold on the concept of FIAT money (money not backed up by Gold) we will continue to see a down spiral movement for the middle class.

You can be sure that if you change your financial mindset from rampant spending to one of cautious spending and even savings, then you will fare better in not only the wake of this terrible financial crisis, but in whatever economic scenario presents itself to you going forward.

Restore Financial Health And Even Attain Financial Fitness

If you are a person who is in debt, and who is struggling under the burden of it, then the Total Money Makeover: A Proven Plan for Financial Fitness is probably for you. The book is authored by Dave Ramsey, who has a wealth of practical experience related to these matters. The author and his work are both considered in the following paragraphs.

About Dave Ramsey the Author

Dave Ramsey proves to be a man who understands how money actually works. He has experienced both the upsides and the downsides of it personally. Having owned and managed a four million dollar valued portfolio of real estate, Dave later ended up filing for bankruptcy before once again achieving the coveted status of millionaire. The man has seen all of the sides of high rolling finance, both good and bad, and lived to tell you about them.

Dave Ramsey learned all about money through painful experience, the hard way. This experience is the elusive underlying factor that has transformed him into a best selling author on the New York Times' list, as well as into a nationally syndicated television and radio host. He has become famed for his advice that some would consider simplistic and old fashioned, much like your grandmother would tell you to do.

His mantras turn out to be live and survive on less money than you actually make, save money as much as you can, and do not get into personal credit card debt.

The Total Money Makeover Book's Premise

True to his no nonsense and straightforward nature and approach to life, Dave Ramsey's Total Money Makeover is exactly what it claims to be. Overflowing with good, solid, and even old fashioned financial advice, his Proven Plan for Financial Fitness is also paired with a number of encouraging tales of the individuals who actually followed his advice to attain financial success.

Some of the subjects in these stories aspired to and reached greatness, while many others are still working on it. Yet all of them prove to be in far better condition now than they were before following his methods, and they all attribute their successes to Dave and his common sense wisdom for first escaping from the prison of debt and then going on to build up wealth.

The book itself is about two subjects, as mentioned. These are how you can get out of debt, and how you can accumulate wealth using simple and basic investments. You will find that it does not get more complicated than these two themes. The author himself claims that that The Total Money Makeover is neither complex nor sophisticated.

He also correctly maintains that his advice for you is not original or unique. The strength of the man and his work instead lies in the fact that he effectively engages you in both a fascinating and encouraging way.

The Total Money Makeover Book's Breakdown

In the start of the book, you quickly see that Dave Ramsey is very negative about debt in all of its many forms. He spends a good amount of time suggesting that you take an honest appraisal of where you are financially and that you do not lie to yourself in the process.

He goes through a number of money and debt myths that actually keep you from attaining a healthy financial state. He also covers several roadblocks that you have to get around in order to achieve your financial goals in life. The first of these is escaping from ignorance. The second is letting go of your old strategy of keeping up with the Joneses.

The Total Money Makeover's Baby Steps

Following these initial mindset changes, Dave encourages you to face your ignorance problems head on using his baby steps plan. The first step in this plan is for you to quickly amass a one thousand dollar emergency pool of money. Once you have achieved this, he has you begin rolling the debt snowball. This concept is not unique to him, as others have suggested it earlier.

It revolves around a system for paying down your smaller debts first before rolling your ex payments forward to tackle the next largest debt until eventually, all of your debt balances are paid down. What he does do well is explain the plan, how it works for you, and its inherent benefits that it offers you. He offers numerous examples to encourage you too.

After you have escaped from debt, Dave Ramsey goes on to give you a plan for paying off your final and largest debt, the mortgage on your house. He then offers practical suggestions for building up your wealth, so that you can live the life of which you have always dreamed. This is not any kind of rocket science manual. But it is extremely effective in its simplicity.

One thing that Dave covers well in this book is the fact that this may be simplistic advice that he is offering you, but it is not easy for you to follow. You can easily grasp his basic concepts. You will not find it simple to put them into practice, particularly if you are among the many legions of Americans who are addicted to spending too much money and utilizing debt to pay for everything. Great discipline is actually required of you to stick with his plan.

A Critique of the Total Money Makeover Book

One charge that critics have leveled at Dave Ramsey and The Total Money Makeover centers around his virulent hatred of both debt and credit. It is easy for you to understand where he is coming from with his entirely negative perception of debt, but debt can have its practical uses that entail benefits.

Many savvy investors utilize debt to build up leveraged investments, such as margin stock or bond portfolios or multiple mortgage properties. In utilizing leverage, you are actually taking on debt to increase your potential profits by obtaining a larger investment than you would be able to without the debt. Corporations and wealthy private investors do this successfully all of the time.

Credit also has its uses when you handle it properly. Using frequent purchasing points from credit cards, you are able to get cash back on purchases, or to work towards significant rewards like airplane tickets. With a twelve or eighteen month no interest charges credit card offer, you can make a larger purchase that you save to pay off before the interest grace period expires.

The key for you in doing these types of things lies in having the discipline to pay them off, so that you do not become burdened down holding a large and draining debt position in the end. Based on the upsetting statistics that Dave offers in the Total Money Makeover though, it is easy to understand why for the majority of Americans, debt is more of a weapon of financial mass destruction than it is a useful tool.

For you who struggle to control your spending and pay down your credit cards after you use them, you should follow his advice in its every small detail.

The end assessment of David Ramsey's The Total Money Makeover: A Proven Plan for Financial Fitness is that for you readers who are struggling beneath a mountain of personal credit card debt, you require some real assistance. If your pay checks are never enough to even keep up with your bills, then his work has some terrific advice to help you. Following it, you can restore your financial health and even attain financial fitness.

It's Just Money - The Phrase That Liberates Or Restrains

There are so many overused cliches on the subject of money. Most of them may be tired, but they generally turn out to be true for the majority of people in many cases. The following paragraphs look at the validity of living you life by these axioms of wisdom, such as "It's Just Money."

Famous Money Axioms

How often have you heard the phrase, "Money does not buy you happiness?" Perhaps you know this famous one, "Money does not grow on trees." No doubt when your finances were temporarily down and out, a friend has given you this comforting one liner before, "Don't take it so hard, it's only money." These often quoted sayings are all true at one time or another, even though they may make good preaching, but hard living, as the phrase goes. Even though you can learn valuable truths from lines such as these, these adages can be not only empowering, but also dangerous.

Take the phrase "Money does not buy you happiness," and analyze this for a moment. Clearly there are many wealthy people in the world, as well as rich and famous Hollywood types, whose lives appear to be a fully chaotic and unhappy mess.

While money may not buy happiness or love though, it does buy practically everything else. Good health, dreams, security, a nice home, possessions, and a car can all be purchased with enough money.

And as for happiness and purpose, if you give enough money to help people in need who are suffering, then you will find that the act of giving away money does bring happiness and also a rewarding sense of purpose. If you have any doubts as to this resulting effect from being generous with money and feeling happiness, then just ask Angelina Jolie, the Hollywood actress who regularly gives away half of her money she makes in a year.

The Liberating Power of the Phrase "It's Just Money"

The wise saying that "it is just money" can be liberating and freeing, especially after you have suffered a financial catastrophe or terrible economic loss. You have seen plenty of reasons for this phrase to be used to comfort people in the last three years. First the global economy fell apart. Then the United States' financial system, and subsequently that of the whole Western world, practically burned to the ground.

Your friends, family, and neighbors, if not you personally, began losing their jobs, their homes, and much of their retirement savings and investment values. There was a sad story of a family in Hong Kong where the husband had become terminally ill and disabled. The wife had put all of their savings, literally everything they had in the world, into some guaranteed Lehman Brothers' structured investments. By now you know the end of that story, along with that poor woman and everyone else.

When Lehman Brothers collapsed with little warning, she and all other Lehman investment holders were totally wiped out. These are people who need the comfort of the phrase "It's only money."

Misery of Being Obsessed with Money

You should know that is it also true that obsession with money can bring misery not only to yourself, but also to your family, and everyone else unfortunate enough to be around you when you are so obsessed.

When you pursue money with single minded purpose, you miss out on meaningful relationships, the subtle and daily joys of life, and finding your ultimate higher purpose in this world. Being obsessed with money is a terrible thing that can wreck your entire existence in the end. Hearing the phrase "it's only money" if you are in this dark place can help you to regain your lost perspective on all the important parts of life.

Acknowledging the Proper Role of Money

Although falling back on the "It's only money" adage has its purposes and times and places, it can also serve to falsely distract you from your financial situation that needs careful management, work, and frequent improvement. You definitely need to countenance the reality at some point that money really does play a critical and meaningful role in your everyday and ongoing life. This is to say that you can not be slack in the proper management of your finances.

The amount of money that you have actually does impact your quality of life in various important ways. The possession of it, or lack thereof, will influence your near, medium, and long term choices, your lifestyle, and even the quality of your health, to name just a few things. If you wish to experience a terrific and full life, then you will have to begin by acting intelligently in the handling of your money and assets.

Tangible Advice for Managing Your Money

It is easy to suffer a serious, or even catastrophic, investment setback and then fall back on the "It's Only Money" argument. But maybe the more useful thing to take away from the tragic and heart breaking experience is not comfort and solace, but an important lesson. Perhaps that investment that you participated in simply entailed way too much risk, even given a potentially impressive return if it worked out in the end.

Maybe the better reaction would be to understand and learn that you should watch very carefully where you put your money. Although you, along with most everyone else out there, may not have realized this before the climactic and traumatic economic events a few years ago, the maximum that you can lose in most investments is everything, one hundred percent. This is true of stocks, bonds, mutual funds, and even guaranteed structured investments of the kind formerly peddled by the likes of Lehman Brothers and Bear Stearns.

"It's only money" as a phrase may bring you comfort in a earth shattering situation like this, but one thing that it will certainly not bring back is the lost money.

But, if you can walk away from such a negative experience as a catastrophic loss in investments and ultimately money having learned an important and valuable lesson for your future money management plans, then maybe the experience will not prove to be in vain, even though you did not escape from the unfortunate consequences that resulted.

Ultimately, you will find that it comes down to this personal reality. You must take your money and financial condition seriously if you are ever going to get anywhere in life. This can be effectively accomplished through learning to be financially savvy about the most efficient ways of managing and even increasing your money.

Learning anything in life comes with a learning curve. Sometimes the curve is minor, and sometimes it turns out to be extremely steep. So when you do run into the inevitable financial and monetary setbacks, be sure to learn a valuable lesson from the hard gained experience. Then you will be able to pick yourself back up off of the ground, dust yourself off, and remind yourself that "It's just money, and I can always make some more."

Why Local Money Is Coming Back to Communities

When you hear about local money making a comeback in communities, you may be confused. You might be led to believe that this means that people are investing their assets in their own local communities.

The phenomenon of local money does not really have much to do with this. Rather, it is all about surviving the ongoing effects of the Great Recession. This concept of local money, along with its history, advantages, successes, and legal issues, is discussed in the following paragraphs.

The Concept of Local Money

It may shock you to learn this, but local money is actually currency that is printed up by local communities. These communities are cash strapped and desperate to improve their hometown situations. Because of this, they have gone back to the concept of creating money that they can keep flowing through businesses in the local area.

The History of Local Money

Local money actually dates back to the dark days of the Great Depression, an era that you, like all Americans, hoped would never come back to haunt the country again. In the Great Depression, banks failed left and right in record numbers. To compensate for the shortages of actual currency flowing through local towns and communities, business and individuals came up with an idea. They decided to band together to create their own currency. This was called Scrip. Using Scrip, commerce was able to keep flowing even when the dwindling numbers of banks led to an actual dollar shortage in smaller towns.

Why Local Money is Making A Comeback

This practice had died out across the country after a normal currency circulation resumed in the U.S. following the end of the Great Depression. But back in 1991, the first major local currency since then was born. This was the Ithaca Hours of Ithaca, New York. BerkShares, the largest such local money currency, was actually created in 2006. Detroit has also launched its own version, the Detroit Cheers.

More are being designed all the time as local communities struggle to find ways to cope with the new economic reality settling over the country. The interest is only increasing as more and more communities struggle to find a way to deal with the after effects of the financial crises and the Great Recession.

How Local Money Actually Works

In order to have a circulating currency, you first have to achieve the cooperation of one or better still several banks.

There is no other practical way to effectively move a currency throughout a community. Next, a large number of businesses have to buy into the concept and agree to accept payment in the form of this new local money currency. Otherwise, local consumers will have no incentive to go out and acquire the local money itself.

This is exactly what is happening in a number of local communities throughout the United States. Businesses in the hundreds are consenting to take the local money currencies. They are then printed up and made available through local area banks. These banks sell this currency at a discount to face value. As an example, a $100 local money bill might be offered by banks for $95 US dollars. The full face value of the currency is then spent at any area business or store that accepts the local money currency.

If this sounds far fetched and unlikely to you, then consider this. Right now, more than a dozen local area communities have their own local money currency that is being accepted on a significant scale. Workers whose paychecks are less and less are using these Ithaca Hours in New York, Detroit Cheers in Illinois, BerkShares in Western Massachusetts, and the Plenty in Pittsboro, North Carolina to pay for grocery store items, gasoline, and even yoga classes.

Benefits to Having a Local Money Currency

You are possibly wondering what is the point of local money currencies, and how they really help out the area in which they are utilized. The idea behind them is two fold. On the one hand, they stretch the purchasing power of consumers who are increasingly struggling to both cover all of their bills and to keep food on the table. On the other hand, they aid local businesses that are struggling to keep the lights on and their employees paid.

Experts in sociology who have studied these local currencies say that they do benefit the local businesses significantly. This is primarily because they motivate local citizens to buy from local area merchants. Since the local currency can not be spent outside of the area locale, the money stays at home in the community. This is a Godsend for area merchants who have suffered terribly as consumers have been forced to reduce their spending since the Great Recession swept over the country back in 2007.

Success of Local Money Currencies

Indeed some of the local currencies have proven to be a smashing success since their inception. Berkshares are available in twelve different local area banks. They can be utilized in three hundred and seventy different area businesses throughout Western Massachusetts.

This largest of local money systems in the United States has already managed to circulate an impressive two million and three hundred thousand dollars of the BerkShares local money. The success of this and other local money currencies has encouraged other areas to try it out. South Bend, Indiana is in the process of launching its own local money currency now.

Legality of Local Money Currency

If you are wondering how these local currencies are allowed to exist, the answer is that Federal law prohibits local money from looking at all like federally issued bills.

It also states that such local currencies may not be advertised as a legal tender of the United States. Only the Bureau of Engraving and Printing is allowed to print the actual national currency.

But, there is no federal statute in place that stops towns or even states from coming up with their own currency to be used alongside the U.S. Dollar. So long as the IRS is paid the appropriate taxes on the use of the money, no laws are being violated. The way these local money currencies work, the business that accepts them must report the income as taxable to the Internal Revenue Service. They do not permit a person or a business to side step national income taxes.

Local Money on a State Level

There is even a state that has joined in the additional currency act. Montana began accepting gold as legal tender for use in everyday purchases in the last few years. Their reasoning for doing this is different from the communities that have begun working with local currency. Montana's government, along with its citizens, were concerned about the U.S. government's continued debasing of the U.S. Dollar as it prints more and more dollars to pay for bailouts and back stop failing investments. So far, this move has been unique to the state of Montana.

The Future of Local Money

You can be sure that businesses like the idea of keeping consumer's money in the local area economy. It helps them to reduce the national impact of the sour economy on the local community. Consumers enjoy effectively stretching their actual purchasing power in the amount of from five to ten percent.

So long as this arrangement continues to benefit both parties in the buying and selling relationship, you will continue to see the rise of still more local money currencies throughout the United States. With the evolving national economic situation that some economists say will never fully recover to pre-Great Recession levels, these local money currencies may be here to stay.

Six Steps to Protect Yourself from Hyperinflation Hardship

In another recent article on this website entitled "What is Hyperinflation and Can it Happen in the US?" you read about the prospects of Hyperinflation affecting the United States in the near future.

If you recall the article, you will remember that hyperinflation has already happened in the United States on three different occasions.

These were back in the Revolutionary and Civil Wars, as well as in 1933 when President Franklin Roosevelt devalued the dollar severely against gold. If double digit inflation or worse breaks out in the American economy over an extended period of time, then you will be far better off if you have taken proactive steps to protect yourself from it.

The following paragraphs discuss these sensible and recommended things that you can do in case significant inflation proves to be in the national future.

A Brief Review of Hyperinflation

For the benefit of you readers who did not read the first article on hyperinflation, a brief review is in order. Hyperinflation is inflation that gets out of control as the prices of all goods and services rise at a rapid pace.

This rate can range from double digit percentage increases to hundreds and even thousands of percentage increases per year. Examples of runaway hyperinflation include Germany following World War I, Hungary after World War II, and Yugoslavia in the 1990's as the country was breaking up. Zimbabwe is presently in the grip of severe hyperinflation.

Some form of hyperinflation is practically assured in the United States as the result of the monetary activities practiced by the Bush and Obama administrations in response to the economic crisis, financial collapse, and Great Recession.

Enormous amounts of money were created from thin air and injected directly into the U.S economy in the final days of President Bush's second term and the first months and year of President Obama's administration. The money supply was increased by as much as three hundred percent in this time frame.

Supply and demand laws tell you that this enormously greater number of dollars chasing the relatively same number of goods and services will lead to massive price increases in the coming months and years. If this does happen, as an increasing number of economists are suggesting, there could be a great deal of poverty and social unrest. This would especially be the case for those living on fixed incomes, such as retirees.

Protecting Yourself from the Hyperinflation

Even in light of these economic revelations, there is no cause for despair. There are a number of proactive steps that you can take to prepare yourself and your family against hyperinflation, as well as to safeguard your wealth. These are detailed in the rest of the article below.

Step #1 - Become More Self Sufficient

If you own a home, then you should endeavor to make it more self sufficient. This can be done by planting some fruit trees in the backyard, and especially by putting in a good vegetable garden. In case the prices of food become too high to bear, at least your family will have a healthy base of food to work off of from your own fresh stock.

It is a good idea to start before the hyperinflation hits, since growing your own food can take some practice and experimentation for it to go as you plan. If they hyperinflation never hits, at least you will be spending more time outdoors enjoying the sunshine and fresh air while you maintain the garden, and you will have the freshest fruits and vegetables on your family table every day.

If starting the vegetable garden or miniature fruit orchard sounds like too much work and trouble, then you can at least prepare yourself against the need by purchasing packages of seeds and bags of soil. If you do this, make sure to buy seeds for plants that grow well in the part of the country in which you live. Then if hyperinflation hits and the inevitable run on gardens supplies happens, you will not be in the stores fighting for the limited packages of seeds.

Step #2 - Create An Emergency Food Supply and Kit

If hyperinflation did happen, then all food costs would increase dramatically. By purchasing a good supply of canned goods and similar non perishable foods, this is one thing that you would not have to worry about for a good amount of time. Having a first aid kit as a part of this is always sensible as well. Even if hyperinflation never materializes, it is always a good idea to have a supply of non perishable food and a first aid kit on hand to be prepared for any disaster or emergency.

Step #3 - Adjust Your Investment Portfolio Now

Once hyperinflation begins, it is already too late to think about your investments. To be prepared for its arrival, you should make some changes to your investments' composition now. Your goal is to protect your investments from the declining purchasing power and value of the U.S. dollar.

One way to do this is to put some of your investment dollars into gold. Regardless of how low the dollar sinks, gold always performs well in such times. Even during the worst of the German hyperinflation, gold had great value and was used to protect many Germans' money. Gold can be bought in coins or bars and conveniently stored in a safe deposit box at your bank, or in a safe at home.

Another way to prepare your portfolio is by purchasing Swiss Francs. Unknown to most people, Switzerland's currency is the only one in the world still backed by gold, as mandated by their constitution. For many centuries, their banks have been safe places to keep money, regardless of the geopolitical situation in Europe and the world. Opening an Swiss Franc account at a Swiss bank is easier than ever, and can even be done over the Internet nowadays.

Step #4 - Reduce Your Debts

Eliminating or at least reducing your outstanding debts is also a good proactive approach to preparing for hyperinflation. The reason for this is that many people will lose their jobs in the economic turmoil that accompanies hyperinflation.

Paying bills would possibly require the little money that you still had coming in. You can start by paying more than the minimum amounts due on all bills.

Finding ways to bring in extra money to pay towards the bills is also advisable. Even if hyperinflation does not happen, you will be better of for getting your finances in better shape.

Step #5 - Have Some Money on Hand Along with Your Critical Documents

You should get all of your critical documents together and have some money at home with them. If hyperinflation led to social unrest in your locale, then you would want to be capable of leaving to go stay with your relatives who live in a more remote area. People outside of the major cities would be likely to have fewer problems in such difficult times. Whether hyperinflation occurs or not, it is always wise to be well prepared for a quick departure in the event of some other emergency or disaster.

Step #6 - Research the Candidates to Vote for the Responsible Ones

One thing that you can still do to help head off hyperinflation lies in researching and voting for the political candidates who comprehend the problems of going down the hyper-inflationary path. It still might not be too late to work to prevent it, if responsible leaders quickly started tackling the runaway money supply increases.

Politicians who are willing to stop printing money and repay part of the national debt are the best choices for this. Be sure to vote against politicians who think that creating money from thin air is perfectly acceptable.

TOOLS

"Instruments for Building a Wealth Foundation"

Ten Interesting and Useful Personal Finance Blogs

Among the hundreds and even thousands of personal financial blogs available on the Internet are a smaller and more select group of those only written by individuals. These cover angles ranging from a mom's point of view, to a debtor's point of view, to a Christian's point of view. The following are ten best financial blogs for you to consider that are actually written by individuals, and not by corporations or committees.

Deal Seeking Mom - Among the Best and Most Popular Personal Money Saving Blogs

This is an infinitely practical blog for you who are looking to save money or even to obtain things for free. Deal seeking mom's blog has a variety of helpful cash saving sections to offer you. These include a coupons group of pages covering everything from a database, to newspaper coupons, to eCoupons, to printable coupons.

You will find an available deals section that covers magazines and books, free music, DVD rentals, restaurant deals, mall deals, photo deals, office supply deals, and online deals. She has a nice freebies section covering kids and babies, food, health and beauty, household items, pet supplies, and organic items.

Besides this, this blog offers you sections on store deals for grocery, mass market retailers, and drugs stores and money making ideas like blogging, paid surveys, and work at home jobs. Her blog ranks at number five from Alexa for popularity and respect of blogging peers. You can check out this imminently practical blog at: http://dealseekingmom.com

Moolanomy - A Family Man's Very Popular Personal Financial Blog

If you are someone who is interested in learning how to escape from debt, increase your money, invest and save towards retirement, make your money work best for you, and increase your skills at investing, then this blog is for you.

The blog author is a thirty-six year old married man who is also a Vice President of a Fairfax, Virgina Internet company. His subjects cover wealth building skills and tools and achieving your financial goals. Although he does not claim to be an expert on finances, or to have any special background in personal finance, his blog is ranked number seven by Alexa Blogging ranking. You can go to read his blog at the link: http://www.moolanomy.com

I will Teach You to Be Rich - A Great Best Selling Author's Blog

This is the personal blog of Ramit Sethi. The writer is the New York Times' listed bestselling author of the book I Will Teach You to Be Rich. He is a Stanford graduate who also co-founded PBwiki.

Among his recent posts is an interesting article about the ways for you to make more money in consulting or freelancing, entitled "How to Go From $25 an Hour to $75 an Hour in Two Weeks". The author has a substantial following, as is evidenced from his number nine ranking from Alexa blog rankings. You can go to his interesting blog by navigating to the following address: http://www.iwillteachyoutoberich.com

Christian PF - the Best Christian Oriented Finance Blog

As you might expect from the title of this personal finance blog, Christian PF is a blog site that features Christian and Bible based context in the practical and helpful financial advice it features. The writer offers you a variety of interesting sub-sections in the blog.

These include budgeting; banking pertaining to CD's, mortgage rates, prepaid credit cards, credit cards, debit cards, and savings rates; debt elimination; insurance, covering home owners insurance, life insurance, auto insurance, and health insurance; making money; investing; saving money; and the Bible and money.

Christian PF is for both people seeking a Bible based approach to money and Christians in need of financial advice. With an Alexa ranking of thirteen, it certainly has a large following and is well regarded by the blogging peers. You can check it out by surfing on over to their blog site at http://www.christianpf.com

20'sMoney - Among the Best Blogs Applicable to Young People

With a goal of teaching young adults how to improve their financial situation to a higher level, 20sMoney is an interesting and helpful personal financial blog. This is not simply a general personal finance blog either.

You will find that it makes the big assumption that you have nailed down all of your personal financial basics and that you are ready to concentrate on higher level subjects pertaining to getting greater returns on your investments, boosting your income, and other economically relevant matters.

If you are a young person who longs to understand how to invest for yourself, if you are a younger adult in reasonably good financial situation and are seeking a higher level with your personal finances, or if you are person who is looking to build other streams of income, then you will find that 20sMoney appeals to you. You can check out 20'sMoney by going over to their blog address at http://20smoney.com

Fund My Mutual Fund - Among the Best Trading and Investing Blogs

For you investors who are neither conservative nor wildly speculative, a terrific trading and investing blog is Fund My Mutual Fund. The site naturally has a model mutual fund that the author references, but you will find that his analysis is fantastic. Mark the author provides in depth and detailed analysis on a number of individual companies and their stocks, along with the wider stock market as well.

He lists out all of his trades for you and also documents his actual performance, which makes this a really useful investing blog. You should read his "Fund My Mutual Fund" blog if you are a person seeking out companies in which to invest that are not the biggest and best known firms.

If you are an individual seeking to understand more about trading and investing, or if you are a person who needs to understand some of the basics regarding technical analysis of stocks and markets. You will find this blog at http://www.fundmymutualfund.com

Early Retirement Extreme - Among the Best Retire Early Blogs

The writer of this unusual blog is a person who chose to retire early on in life via radically cutting his expenses to a minimal amount. He did this so he could afford to live off of the money that he had saved when he was working.

The writer tells you about his path to financial independence that he achieved through aggressively saving most of his earnings for a few years and then trading in his materialistic style of life for a more frugal and freer one. He also gives you helpful advice for saving money in several different areas of your life. If you are a person who wishes to retire early or who wants to learn to live more frugally, then you will enjoy this blog. It is available at http://earlyretirementextreme.com

Darwin's Finance - Among the Best ETF Blogs

If you are one of those people who loves Exchange Traded Funds and can not get enough of them, or who simply wants to better understand ETF's, then you should look into Darwin's Finance. The writer concentrates on personal finance topics as well, yet still somehow manages to tie them into the number of high quality ETF possibilities available to you the investor. You can read all about this subject as it relates to your personal finances by going to http://www.darwinsfinance.com

Debt Kid - Among the Best Getting Out Of Debt Stories & Blogs

The writer of this amazing subject blog began his story with $300,000 in personal debt. He is busy getting out of that personal financial mess towards financial prosperity. In his interesting blog, you will read about some terrific personal financial subjects and stories. If you are looking to escape form debt or to get suggestions from someone who has been in the trenches, then you should go over to his blog found at http://www.debtkid.com

FruGal - Among the Best Personal Finance Blogs Written From A Female Point of View

If you read much about personal finance, then you will see that men mostly populate the field. This blog is unusual in that it is written by a woman. Her content and subjects prove to be unique. If you are either a woman or a person who wants a different take on personal finance, then hurry on over to her blog at http://www.-totallymoney.com/frugal/

Rich Dad Education - Learn
To Be Rich Workshop Review

My wife and I just came back from a free two-hour seminar provided by Rich Dad Education. The presentation speaker was Rodney Huffman, long associated with Rich Dad Education as a featured presenter.

These 2 hour free training workshops are popping up more and more as Robert Kiyosaki, the author of Rich Dad, Poor Dad extends his financial philosophy to his circle of followers.

Current popularity of these events suggest that Robert and his wife Kim have at least partially succeeded in expanding the scope of the original book to others interested in building upon their initial enthusiasm about the book.

Rich Dad, Poor Dad establishes Kiyosaki's unique credentials as an in-the-know investor who was the product of two very different upbringings, one from a rich dad and one from a poor one. Robert eventually learned to obtain the advice of each of them and compare them in a kind of homegrown test of his own design: Which dad's philosophy turned out to be successful in terms of a fuller engagement with life and which one failed?

The Huffman seminar had been advertised as free and a lot of extras were thrown in like a bonus audio CD and a DVD. As expected, there was a pitch made to up-sell the participants with a more comprehensive - and costly - package.

It turned out that this 2 hour class was about real estate, which is actually the market where Robert Kiyosaki created his fortune and where he is now showing the public how to duplicate his success in this area.

Am I a bit skeptical? You bet! I am wary of these so-called free seminars that turn out, in the end, to be short on substance and long on sales pitch. I want value right from the start but American business culture being what it is, you can actually learn something even at these events if you can put your doubts aside briefly and listen to the basic message with an open ear.

Huffman started his presentation with The Five Keys to Being Wealthy:

- Do I always feel as though I am behind in my work?
- Do I want myself and my team to be more productive?
- Do I need to find a balance between work and home?
- Do my team members shirk from responsibility?
- Do I struggle with distractions?
- Do I work for a business with frequent turnaround of employees?

Millions of people these days are forced to allow foreclosure on their home or property. That's one side of the coin. The other side buys it for pennies on the dollar. Kiyosaki has made a fortune by continuing to point out that the greatest fear of the American people right now is their fear of not having enough money when they retire. A USA Today poll shows that the number of people is almost 70 percent.

As Huffman illustrated in the seminar, what better way to avoid foreclosure in the first case is to have enough liquidity to handle your existing mortgage? And, on the other side of the coin, opportunities abound in the current market for investing in good properties for pennies on the dollar. For the smart investor, this is a good way to realize significant gains in the market. For everyone else, the current downward trend will result - or already has resulted - in disaster.

Most people would like to be rich, of course, but have never learned anything about what it takes to invest successfully. Our educational system doesn't help: people are not trained to keep their minds sharp and engaged in learning complex new things; they are trained to be cogs in a system that values uniformity, not brilliant analysis and decisive problem solving. It's not easy to change these lazy mental habits once they've been allowed to take gather cobwebs for 20 or 30 years.

Wealthy investors are sharp investors. Poor ones have lost their focus

Another telling difference between wealthy and poor people is that wealthy people plan for the long term - for generations if need be; poor people barely manage to plan for Saturday night. It's the degree of skill involved in strategic planning for extended periods of time that set the two apart. What does it take to be wealthy? Surely not just strategic planning. Huffman spoke about the several elements found in the:

Millionaire Mindset

- The European countries involved in WWII were heavily in debt to the US.
- The US economy was very strong and the value of dollar had appreciated.
- Of all the major world currencies, only the US dollar was backed by gold.
- The US agreed to link the dollar to the gold price of $35 per ounce and exchange gold bullion for dollars.

There are three steps to success:

- Do I always feel as though I am behind in my work?
- Do I want myself and my team to be more productive?
- Do I need to find a balance between work and home?
- Do my team members shirk from responsibility?
- Do I struggle with distractions?
- Do I work for a business with frequent turnaround of employees?

Seeing and recognizing the opportunity, having the knowledge to understand what it means and finally acting on it to make it real. Thus the Millionaire Mindset is realized in real terms through real actions.

Huffman then launched into his big pitch, which involves a three-day real estate seminar held in various places during the coming weeks. This seminar is focused on buying cheap properties that are either close to foreclosure or already in foreclosure, and in auction.

The interesting thing about this kind of investing is that banks are generally not needed to finance these opportunistic investments. As you may know, banks now have much more stringent lending requirements than just four or five years ago when so-called "ninja loans" were common. Ninja loans are basically loans that get approved even when the investor does not have the financial stability and income to be fully qualified. Four of five years ago any janitor making $10 an hour could get a house loan with zero money down.

Why is the real estate market such a great opportunity right now? It's shaping up to be the vehicle for the single largest upcoming wealth transfer in history. First of all, interest rates are at historic lows - and are not likely to get any lower. Secondly, foreclosure rates are skyrocketing. Thirdly, the demand for people wanting to live in their own homes is high and getting higher. All together, these factors add up to a huge, mostly untapped market with massive investment potential.

The three-day seminar promises the keys to picking good, equity-rich properties, and how to finance them without relying on your own money or on trying to get money from the bank. Perhaps most importantly of all, the three-day seminar promised to outline the details of how to construct a viable exit plan that takes into account fluctuating market conditions.

Some viable exit strategies:

- The European countries involved in WWII were heavily in debt to the US.
- The US economy was very strong and the value of dollar had appreciated.
- Of all the major world currencies, only the US dollar was backed by gold.

- The US agreed to link the dollar to the gold price of $35 per ounce and exchange gold bullion for dollars.

There are probably a lot more but that's all what Rodney revealed. There are more details surrounding the three-day seminar, but Huffman remained mostly silent on that subject while occasionally throwing out tidbits like: never buying investment properties in your own name, real estate tax advantages for investors, and leveling up to better properties rather than cashing out.

Sitting through the mini-seminar, I recalled one item about how Robert Kiyosaki bought a 300-unit apartment complex using 90 percent financing with other people's money. After minor improvements, he refinanced the property, recouped his down payment and went on to make $20,000 per month in passive income.

These and similar tales are all the inducement approximately 50 percent of the mini-seminar's audience needed to take the plunge on the three-day event. Of course, the price was attractive too - just $199 for you and a friend or spouse, reduced from the usual $1000 or more.

My wife Aviva and I really enjoyed this mini-seminar and we are excited about the opportunity it presents to learn more about maximizing investment potential in today's real estate market. Our seminar engagement date is in October and I will keep you posted on our experiences and conclusions.

The 10 Best Financial Applications For Your iPad

The Apple iPad is the hottest product on the computer market. The iPad offers great potential especially for apps designed to take advantage of it architecture and its many features.

All of the built-in apps on iPad were designed from the ground up to take advantage of the large Multi-Touch screen and advanced capabilities of iPad. And they work in any orientation. So you can do things with these apps that you can't do on any other device.

These financial apps include both paid and free apps that are highest rated apps available in the Apple Apps Store.

Best Paid Financial Apps

Budgets for iPad (with Sync)

Budgets for iPad (with Sync) is an iPad app designed to handle and track all your budgeting needs. The futuristic design of the app is geared to take advantage of the iPad interface. It features detailed management of different budget categories, highly detailed entries that allow the user to select the periodicity and time window, and it offers a variety of charts and graphs.

The Budgets for iPad app sells for $0.99 and was rated 3 out of 5 stars in the Apps Store. It has security features that let the user set a PIN code for access. The app allows the user to sync their data with other iPads. Data can be exported to HTML and CSV formats.

http://ibearsoft.com/

Bills for iPad (with Sync)

Bills for iPad is another financial app that is developed by iBear-Soft for the iPad. The app tracks monthly bills and expenses and helps the user control the amount of their monthly spending. Bills for iPad can filter the payments based on bills paid, bills planned, and bills that are overdue.

Information can be displayed in a calendar view or in a list view on an interface that is specially designed for the iPad. This app also allows the user to sync their data with other iPads. Data in Bills for iPad can be exported to HTML and CSV formats. Bills for iPad is available in the Apps Store for $0.99 and was rated 3 out of 5 stars.

http://ibearsoft.com/

Expense Tablet for iPad

Expense Tablet for iPad is a budget manager and personal expense tracker that provides a simple to use interface. It allows the user to track expenses by category and by account on a monthly basis.

When using the app in landscape mode, it presents history graphs for each account and each category. It has PIN number security protection. Expense Tablet for iPad sells for $0.99 in the apps store. It was rated 3 out of 5 stars with over 100 ratings.

http://adamcode.com/

Market Scan

Market Scan is a financial app developed for the iPad that allows you to track stocks through multiple sites such as Yahoo Finance, Google Finance, CNBC, MSN Money, Bloomberg, and others. It comes pre-loaded with those sites previously mentioned and three others. Other sites can be added or deleted.

Market Scan also allows you to track market indices, mutual funds, and other components that have a symbol. Information from these sites can be news, charts, commentary, and other financial information. The app sells for $3.99 in the Apps store and is rated 3 stars.

http://www.makosoftware.com

Fiscal

Fiscal is an iPad app that presents stocks and other investments that are kept in Google Finance. Stock prices are constantly updated and is reflected in the app by glowing LED stock symbols.

Graphs, charts, and tables are available to display the stock prices and information. With the consolidated view in Fiscal, all share prices can display across all portfolios. Historical data is cached and made available for viewing offline. Fiscal sells for $4.99 in the Apps store. It is rated 2 stars.

http://www.padvance.com/app/fiscal

Best Free Financial Apps

FXware

FXware is an iPad application that is targeted towards global investors, global travelers, and those who have an interest in international currencies and world markets. The app provides access to currency exchange rates for more than 160 currencies and commodities.

The free app provides access to the latest forex market news, world indices, and the latest development occurring in the global world markets. FXware includes an integrated currency converter, historical trend charts, and daily rankings. FXware is rated 4 stars in the Apps store.

http://www.fxware.com/ipad

Thomson Reuters Marketboard

Thomson Reuters Marketboard is a new app designed for the iPad that provides a visual display of financial information. This app takes advantage of the larger format available with the iPad as opposed to using a smartphone's smaller screen. The touch screen feature provides an experience that also differs from accessing financial information on a laptop.

This free app allows users, that include financial professionals, students, and investors to read financial charts, download pdf files, and access other financial information. It also has a core screen to view interactive info and a virtual briefcase where offline information and data can be read. Thomson Reuters Marketboard is rated 3 stars in the Apps store with over 700 ratings.

http://www.thomsonreuters.com

QFolio HD - NASDAQ OMX Portfolio Manager

QFolio HD - NASDAQ OMX Portfolio Manager is a financial app for the iPad that allows the user to obtain real time quotes from U.S., Nordic, and Baltic stocks. This free iPad app has other features including multiple watch lists, StockTwits TV and Real Time Conversation Streams, charting features, and ticker with recent trades.

Users can also create virtual portfolios of their favorite stocks. QFolio HD - NASDAQ OMX Portfolio Manager is rated 2.5 stars with over 500 ratings from users in the App store.

http://www.nasdaqomx.com/whoweare/qhappenings/ipad/

Bloomberg for iPad

Bloomberg for iPad is a free app designed specifically for the iPad. It offers news, stock quotes, company information, price charts, market analysis, and other financial information.

This app allows the user to create custom charts of their favorite stocks, receive financial podcasts, access currency information, monitor commodity prices, and share news articles via e-mail. The app is one of the top rated by over 1800 users in the App store. It received 3.5 stars out of 5.

http://www.bloomberg.com/

Investment Guide By Forbes

Investment Guide + By Forbes is an app for the iPad made available by the publishers of Forbes Magazine. This free app provides financial advice for families and individuals who need assistance sorting out all the financial information that can be confusing and complex. The Investment Guide app provides news articles and information that is presented well on the iPad.

Information covers personal and home finance, investing, taxes, and other areas of finance helpful to the layman. Articles can be shared with others through the use of e-mail and can also be read offline. The app is rated 2.5 and has over 600 ratings in the Apps store.

http://www.forbes.com/iPad

The 10 Best Financial Applications For Your iPhone

Managing personal finances is one of the most time-consuming tasks for many people. Using the Apple iPhone to help streamline the task has never been easier with the many available financial applications for the iPhone.

The following list provides the best financial apps for the iPhone to help manage budgets, track income and expenses, and handle other financial management activities.

These financial apps include both paid and free apps that are highest rated apps available in the Apple Apps Store.

Best Paid Financial iPhone Apps

BillTracker

BillTracker is a financial application that helps you manage your bills. The app developed by SnapTap is a popular app that sells for $1.99 in the Apple App Store. The features of BillTracker include the ability to track information for each bill, track account information, due date reminder, creation of recurring bills, currency selector, historical bill information, and calendar views to highlight when bills are due.

Accounts can be called from the phone numbers stored in Bill-Tracker and new accounts can be opened from the iPhone. Its robust features with a straightforward interface make it one of the most popular financial apps. BillTracker received 4 stars from over 4 thousand ratings.

http://snaptapapps.com

Ace Budget

For the low cost of $0.99, the Ace Budget financial app is an excellent investment. Rated 4.5 stars, it offers features to help track and manage expenses and income. It provides the flexibility to create daily, weekly, biweekly, monthly, semi-monthly, quarterly, and annual budgets.

The Ace Budget apps provides charts and reports, reminders, scheduling of recurring payments, budget history, transferring between categories, and CSV exporting of data.

Transfers of transactions via e-mail to other iPhone users with Ace Budget can be done. Other features include a quick entry list, search, and autocomplete. With its clean and intuitive user interface, Ace Budget is one of best financial apps for the iPhone.

http://www.svtsoftware.com

iXpenseIt

iXpenseIt is a great iPhone app to keep track of expenses but personal and business. As one of the most popular financial apps as rated by CNN Money Magazine, Laptop Magazine, and PC World, it received 4 stars in the Apple Apps Store.

iXpenseIt allows users to track income and cash flow, store digital photo receipts, generate graphical reports, generate expense summaries, track mileage, and import/export the data in a csv or html format via e-mail or Wi-Fi.

The reporting features of iXpenseIt are very robust. Reports can be created by various criteria such as payment, vendor, dates, etc. iXpenseIt offers backup and restore to help protect your data. This app is available in 12 languages, has a built-in currency converter, and it sells for $4.99.

http://www.ixpenseit.com

Loan Calculator Pro

Loan Calculator Pro is another iPhone app by SVT Software. It is a financial calculator that is very user-friendly. This financial app is rated 4.5 stars and sells for only $0.99 but has a lot of features.

In addition to providing the standard loan and mortgage calculations it also allows the users to do "what if" scenarios to determine early payoff and interest savings.

It has an early payoff simulation, extra payment tracking, amortization table, bookmarking feature, and e-mail export. One great feature of Loan Calculator Pro is the ability to save multiple loans and the "what if" scenarios. The app even has a large numeric keyboard to help make numeric entries easier.

http://www.svtsoftware.com

DebtTracker Pro

For those wanting to get a handle on managing their debt, Debt-Tracker Pro is one of the best financial applications for the iPhone to help achieve that task. DebtTracker Pro allows the user to track their credit balance, credit lines, payment due date, payment history, and several other metrics.

Users can develop a payoff plan that will help them quickly reduce their debt. It has the ability to create "what if" scenarios by adjusting the payments to determine the overall time to payoff a particular debt.

DebtTracker Pro uses the debt snowball system developed by Dave Ramsey. Other features include payment date reminders, password protection, and currency selection. The app costs $2.99 and is rated 4 stars with over 1000 ratings. This is another great financial app from SnapTap.

http://snaptapapps.com

Best Free Financial iPhone Apps

Mint.com Personal

Mint.com Personal is a money management app that allows the user to track, budget, and manage their money directly from their iPhone. Mint.com Personal can automatically sync with online banking and investment accounts to pull the data directly into the app.

The app displays monthly spending, budgets, and investments.

It will organize spending by categories to help make budget management a snap. Users will have to sign up for a Mint.com account in order to use the iPhone application. Mint.com Personal received 4 stars on the Apple Apps Store site. Highly recommended by other sites such as Bankrate.com, it is one of the best financial management apps available for the iPhone.

http://www.mint.com

Bloomberg

To obtain real-time financial market news, corporate information, stock quotes, national and world financial headlines, and other financial information, you can't beat the free Bloomberg financial app. Commodity information, bonds, and equity indices are also available through the app.

Breaking news, interactive charts, and the ability to track your personal stocks makes this a must-have app. The Bloomberg app received a rating of 4 stars in the Apple App Store.

http://www.bloomberg.com/mobile

E*TRADE Mobile Pro

Offering many of the same features as the computer website, E*TRADE Mobile Pro is another free financial app that offers features often found in a paid application. Users will find that it offers real-time quotes, graphical and historical charts, breaking market news, account management, stocks and options trading, and stock price alerts.

The app also offers the Quick Transfer feature which will let you easily transfer cash from one institution to another. Rated 4 stars with over 1100 ratings, E*TRADE Mobile Pro is one of the best financial apps for the iPhone.

https://us.etrade.com/e/t/mobile_pro/iphone

Discover Mobile

Rated as one of the best financial applications for the iPhone, Discover Mobile is a favorite by its users. Rated 4.5 stars with over 3,000 ratings, it has features to put your Discover account management right at your fingertips. The app offers robust account management, bill payment, rewards management, payment notifications feature, and easy navigation.

The app offers password protection and security to protect the users personal information. Discover Mobile is one of the best banking and financial apps available for the iPhone.

http://www.discovercard.com/customer-service/account/mobile.html

Pageonce Personal Finance

This highly rated and free personal finance app is one of the best financial applications for the iPhone. Developed by Pageonce, Inc., the app allows users to manage all of their online accounts from credit cards, bank accounts, investment portfolios, mobile phone minutes, and even frequent flyer accounts.

Pageonce Personal Finance is a great way to have all of your account balances in one place. It offers graphs and historical payment tracking to help manage your expenses and debt. Pageonce Personal Finance is rated 3.5 stars in the Apple App Store and is highly recommended by such entities as New York Times, USA Today, CNET, Fox News, and PC Magazine.

http://www.pageonce.com

WORKING

"Moving Towards Passioned Contribution"

Working

The Way We Are Working Isn't Working Anymore

"The Way We're Working Isn't Working Anymore: The Four Forgotten Needs that Energize Great Performance" By Tony Schwartz

While this book reads like a self-help book, it gives the necessary information to create a successful business. Whether the reader is a low-ranking employee or top dog in the company, there are valuable lessons between the pages of Tony Schwartz's latest book. Even though they seem profound, they are relatively simple answers as to how to get by in such a complex, fast-paced, money-driven society.

Many people will pick up this book and feel as though it does not apply to them. Before they put it back down, they should ask themselves a few questions:

- Do I always feel as though I am behind in my work?
- Do I want myself and my team to be more productive?
- Do I need to find a balance between work and home?
- Do my team members shirk from responsibility?
- Do I struggle with distractions?
- Do I work for a business with frequent turnaround of employees?

If someone can answer "yes" to even one of these questions, for the small fee of a book, they can turn their live around.

Part One: A New Way of Working

The first part of Schwartz's "The Way We're Working Isn't Working" is not a lesson on how to reach the enlightenment he is offering. What would parts two through five have to offer? Instead, the section entitled "A New Way of Working" takes a look at the way the working world has evolved over the years, decade, and centuries.

There are so many things that are new to the business world that we do not even notice, and what we don't notice, we can't change. Because we are such creatures of habit, we need to acknowledge that some of the actions we take on a daily basis for no other reason than "that's just how it's done" may add to the stress and headache. Think for a second: How many times a day do you check your email? Schwartz wants his readers to understand the working life before he embarks on his "Four Forgotten Needs."

Part Two: Sustainability/Physical

Part Two begins with the first forgotten need. Sustainability is the need that is often never overlooked. Everybody is concerned with their next paycheck to sustain themselves. However, people often overlook the physical aspect of their job. Some readers may be thinking, "I work in an office.

It doesn't get physical until the copier has a paper jam." That is not the kind of physical Schwartz is referring to. Even if a job means never leaving a desk, there should be that moment that makes the worker's heart start pumping out of excitement or adrenaline. A job that does not captivate in body and mind needs to be altered. Schwartz explains how to create this union that most people lack.

Part Three: Security/Emotional

Most workers understand the concept of security. Unfortunately, most do not actually get to experience it in the financial sense. While Schwartz is a highly intelligent man, he does not have the capability to get his readers a raise overnight. So, if someone cannot be financially secure, they should at least be emotionally secure in their position.

A big point that Schwartz makes is the distinction between facts and stories that people tell themselves. For example, someone can tell the "story" of how fulfilling their career is while the "fact" is that they count down seconds until five o'clock. This simple example is just the tip of the iceberg. In his book, Schwartz helps the readers find a sense of emotional security in a job that may merely be a means of financial security, if even that.

Part Four: Self-Expression/Mental

It's the American dream. When someone loves a job and can use it to express their natural talents, their self-expression becomes a source of income. If this was the case for everyone, Schwartz would have nothing to write about. He does not recommend quitting the long-established career life to pursue a passion for juggling.

We've all heard the phrase, "When you can't be with the one you love, love the one you're with." In this case, it has nothing to do with romance. Employees cannot change their bosses to suit their needs, but they can make minor adjustments in their own life that will have a substantial difference on their mind. It's not about engaging the brain more; it's about using it effectively, which just so happens to mean sometimes using it less.

Part Five: Significance/Spiritual

Spirituality is often separated from the workplace. This helps to keep office drama to minimum and avoid unnecessary conflicts. While it is not the place to hold a daily service or pass out pamphlets, there is a bit of spirituality that is welcomed and essential in the office. It is more of a personal spirituality.

It is important to ask yourself what you really want. In extreme cases, combining every idea, tip, and guideline that Schwartz has to offer will still leave some in a miserable situation with hopeful coping mechanisms. Schwartz can help his readers figure out whether it is the attitude toward the job or the job itself that is causing stress and frustration.

Significance and spirituality has another purpose in the office. When employees must work together on a project, they need to embody the same relative feelings toward it. If a few are working hard, a few are staring at the clock, and the middle ground is keeping themselves occupied with meaningless "busy work," there is bound to be tension and unproductivity. Schwartz can help readers learn how to provoke some purpose into their coworkers who have not yet gotten to his book. It is not a cure-all for them, but it can help make your life easier if only for the few hours of collaboration.

Not Just for Suits and Ties

Schwartz's book may appeal to the businessmen and businesswomen of society, but the help he gives can apply to much more. Parents, teachers, and spouses can use the profound information in their relationships to ease tension and create a peaceful environment in the classroom or home. Schwartz's book is an all-encompassing, non-exclusive key to happiness and satisfaction.

From Employee to Entrepreneur in 5 Steps

Do you dream of owning your own business? Setting your own hours? Working only for yourself and your family? Do you feel like you are an employee trapped in an entrepreneur's body?

Entrepreneurs are common people like you and I, who have a driving ambition and vision of what they want to create, whether it is a product or a service. Taking the risk of becoming an entrepreneur requires an unflagging dedication to success without being impeded by the fear of failure.

From the moment we are very young, we are taught to be afraid of making mistakes and try to protect ourselves from uncertainty. Entrepreneurs create their own place in the marketplace and usually take a completely creative approach to the product or service they are offering. They are creative and ambitious in the way they approach sales and product development.

An entrepreneur is an individual who is able to adapt new ideas to a relevant marketplace in order to make money. A successful entrepreneur does not rely on luck alone, but is an intelligent business person who works diligently and makes smart choices with his or her vision in mind.

Step One: Clarify Your Goals

The transition from employee to entrepreneur may be somewhat difficult when you're not sure what to expect. The first thing to do is to make sure you have well-defined goals and know what your motivation is for pursuing your business goals. This clarity will keep you motivated when times become difficult and you feel things have started to crawl at an unbearable pace. At times, you may even feel that every obstacle imaginable is in your path to success. Being clear about your initial vision and motivation to launch a successful business will keep you focused and motivated during the leaner times.

Step Two: Create A Consistent Schedule

Now that you are your own boss, there is no one telling you what to do or when to do it, you can work whenever and wherever you want. One of the first things you want to do is set a timetable, hours of operation as it were, so that you and customers know when you are open. It could be 11-2 or 6-9, or both, whatever you want. It's your own business and you are your own boss. Beware of the common traps people often fall into. It's not Guinness time! Your company will only pay you for the efforts you make to produce a profit.

Watch out for the bane of every self-employed entrepreneur, procrastination. For example, many people idle away the time in unproductive activities such as sharpening the pencil, organizing all of their paperwork on their desk, making sure the computer cables and screen are nice and clean and so on.

While these are things that you may want to take care of, you will not be paid any money for completing such tasks! It is very important, especially in the first few years of you business, to participate in income generating activities during your business hours, such as talking with potential customers, putting ads online or in the local newspaper, doing market research and so on.

Step Three: Find A Mentor

A great support for the new entrepreneur is to find a mentor who is already getting the results you seek. This is someone who can help you establish a plan for success in your business. He or she will be able to offer you insight and suggestions on marketing strategies, organizational infrastructure and continued product or service development.

Step Four: Believe In Your Product Or Service

Please ensure that the products or services you are marketing are items you can be proud of and have the desire to share with others. You must believe in what you are selling. You have to feel excited and good about what you are offering your customers, so that they also become excited about your product or service and want to purchase it.

Step Five: Have A Sustainable Marketing Plan

It is important to make sure that you have a simple marketing system that can run consistently and reliably.

Begin by determining a percentage of your gross income that you will invest monthly in your marketing campaign and then consistently re-invest it in your marketing system. Again, this takes you back to your mentor, who will help teach you what to do in order to succeed.

Now, imagine having all the pieces in place. You do not have to know all the answers immediately, but it helps to be sure you've done your due diligence on starting your business. Talk to others who are in the same business and pick their brains. Do not be afraid to ask questions and get help. You will be amazed at how much people are willing to help, if you ask.

Three Great Benefits of Being An Entrepreneur

1. Being In Control:

One of the best aspects of being an entrepreneur is that you have absolute control of your life. You can work your own hours and determine the tasks you want to focus on. You can also take a vacation any time you feel that you would like one. You can decide what happens in your company. Best of all, nobody can fire you! It totally rocks to be your own boss and create your own destiny.

2. The Work Is Fun:

Now, most people working in 9-5 jobs are always exhausted at the end of the day and are dreading the next morning, especially after the weekend. Some call it the "Monday Morning Blues." An entrepreneur works 24/7 and therefore puts all their energy into their work.

By working this hard, he or she is taking all the risk but is also acquiring all the profit and that's challenging, exciting and fun.

3. Freedom From Boredom

A great German thinker and philosopher, Arthur Schopenhauer, says there are two types of misery. One is the misery of the working class and the other is the boredom of fashionable society.

The misery of the working class is situated on the fact that these people are busy creating wealth for others, not themselves. They are often compensated only enough to keep a roof over their heads and food on the table, not thrive. They want to enjoy life, but are very constrained by the limits of their work schedule and salary.

On the other hand, the misery of fashionable society is that once you have "made it" and are able to all the things a typical "working class" person dreams of doing, after a while, it becomes boring. Imagine doing the same things over and over in a dull monotone. Eventually a life of leisure usually enters a state of ennui, a state of absolute boredom.

Usually a business person who becomes rich is not primarily involved in his endeavor to enjoy the pleasures of the rich. Getting to execute their ideas is what satisfies him or her. For a true entrepreneur, work is not a means to an end. It is an end in itself.

The process is as rewarding to the entrepreneur as the final product. Because an entrepreneur is consumed by his or her desire to work hard and creatively, they really have no time to engage in the trivialities of everyday life and are too busy to sweat the small stuff.

WEALTH

"Pursuing Prosperity with Financial Education"

Wealth Is More Than A Mindset

"Creating Wealth - Retire in Ten Years," by Robert G. Allen, is written in a very relaxed, conversational tone that anyone can relate to. It is almost like the author is sitting right across from you in a casual discussion at your dinner table. He has a wealth of information providing numerous metaphors, comparisons, and stories that prove his points.

Robert G. Allen has a good organizational structure for his wealth-creating book: Foundations, Automatic-Pilot Principles, Timing, Risk/Reward Ratios, and the Proper Mindset. His chapters provide more specific examples within each of these larger categories. "Creating Wealth" covers the spectrum from restrictive fallacies that keep people poor to specific strategies to generate wealth.

Pillars of Strength

Robert G. Allen begins by breaking down the fallacies that hold us back from generating wealth. He explains that many of these ideas have an ounce of truth in them, but lead to a defensive mentality that doesn't take risks.

Who doesn't want to be wealthy? Everyone wants to be wealthy, yet few succeed. Why do some men have more wealth than they will every need, while others starve in poverty? What are the secrets to wealth creation?

"Creating Wealth" continually encourages readers to ask themselves the same question - "Do the wealthy follow such-and-such a strategy?" Robert G. Allen shows readers that there are concrete methods to wealth creation.

Automatic Wealth Generation

F. Scott Fitzgerald said, "The rich are different from you and me."

Some people will argue about what that means exactly, but won't disagree with the basic premise. Have you ever wondered why so many of the wealthy seem to be on vacation all the time. Somehow, they continue to generate wealth. How do they do it?

Robert G. Allen talks about the stages of wealth. The final goal is to be in a position to enact the "Automatic-Pilot Principle."

Just like poker, wealth creation is about managing your assets to the maximum. The best poker players are always calculating odds, looking towards the future, and measuring the value of their assets. They maximize the potential of every hand.

Creating wealth is about optimizing our assets so that we can gain higher levels of leverage and control. The wealthy have good discipline in using proper actions to take advantage of opportunities for acquiring more wealth. They see opportunities that others miss.

They do not waste their time with fruitless pursuits. They cut their losses before they lose everything. They anticipate the future. They set goals, visualize and determine the risk-reward probability of success.

Robert G. Allen shares his "Seven Principles of Wealth," which combine the most important facets for controlling wealth.

Timing

While some professors might talk theoretically about wealth creation, Robert G. Allen puts his money where his mouth is. He has challenged anyone to give him a small amount of money and transport him to any city in the United States - and in 72 hours he will purchase real estate with little money down. Read the book to see if he succeeds at this challenge.

The wealthy have a different mindset that anticipates opportunities. Many poor people lament about the latest success stories - stocks, real estate, and commodities - telling themselves that they would be rich if they had invested at the beginning of a trend cycle. The funniest thing is that when you start talking about the next "big thing" and ask them how they plan to take advantage of it - their response is exactly the same as when they missed their last opportunity. They refuse to learn.

Robert G. Allen continually compares foolish habits of the poor versus wise habits of the wealthy in articulating his point. Wealth creation demands proper thought processes; after failure there needs to be a learning process.

There are many gems of wisdom in this book that are well-worth the purchase price. Robert G. Allen goes through "Eight Cookie Cutters" that provide different strategies for succeeding in real estate. Learn about scoring mortgages, diversification, and compound interest. Learn the basic steps to dealing with problems.

Robert G. Allen is honest about the pitfalls of debt. He asserts the importance of leveraging your assets to generate wealth. He even include basic forms for landlords too.

Risk versus Reward Calculation

The wealthy don't gamble, they calculate the proper risk versus reward ratio. Interest measures the risk involved with any investment by assigning the proper reward. The wealthy are able to properly measure how different events will affect their financial assets.

Robert G. Allen discusses a variety of different financial assets: gold, coins, real estate, and money market funds. Discover the different types of wealth and how they differ in terms of liquidity, hedging, and historical rate of return. For each investment, he calculates how different interest rates will affect wealth accumulation.

What is Wealth?

Whereas, most people believe that wealth is merely money, Robert G. Allen explains that wealth is more of a mindset. The wealthy are in a position to use their excess money (profits) to leverage their investments. The powerful use money to increase their power and vice versa.

While the poor might have the mentality - "You are what you eat." The wealthy believe that "You are what you think." Robert G. Allen explains how "mental work" can control "physical work." Robert G. Allen concludes the book with a list of inspirational quotes from the successful.

Whether you want to understand the general concepts of the wealthy or learn specific details about real estate, Robert G. Allen's "Creating Wealth - Retire in Ten Years" has the information you need. It is a great read, keeping you interested and entertained. With this great wealth creation book, you will be able to develop the proper thought processes, mindsets, and habits to be successful.

Instant Gratification - The Downfall to Building Wealth

How did we become a generation that wants things now, no matter what? It seems as if instant gratification is ingrained in us. The recent economic downturn has made us aware of this fact. This mindset affects virtually every aspect of our lives. Our grandparents were a generation of savers but it seems we are a generation of spenders.

How many people do you know who are looking for the next get rich quick scheme? They are the ones that want to be shown through a video or online webinar how to get rich overnight instead of learning solid business techniques they can apply to build a successful business. They are seeking instant gratification in their professional and personal lives.

They are also the people who spend hundreds of dollars on games, gels, and even botox to gain instant youth the minute they see a gray hair or wrinkle in the mirror. Are they vain or is it simply that we live by instant gratification.

Most of us believe that faster is definitely better and slow is inefficient. We live in the fast lane, enjoy fast food, demand fast service, and expect fast technology. We want it now!

So How Did We Get Here?

Some people feel that technology plays an important role in this instant gratification syndrome. Technology offers a way to do more in less time. We can communicate with one another instantly through texting, e-mail, cell phones, and social networks like Twitter and Facebook.

Industry exploits our instant gratification. We are not only inundated by billboards on every highway, but besieged with advertising on every website we visit. Each message tries to stimulate us to impulse buy.

Before the current economic downturn, credit card companies offered high credit limits while realtors and financial institutions qualified homeowners for houses they could not afford. They were selling the American dream and we bought into it. Their mantra was, why wait when you can have it now? Or, buy now, pay later!

How Has Instant Gratification Affected our Monetary System?

Our current economic downturn is global and affects all of us. Governments have overspent to the point of bankruptcy in some cases while banks, financial institutions, and even private business have liquidated assets. Our society has a high unemployment rate forcing many to start living within their means, sometimes for the first time in their lives.

Has Instant Gratification Put You In Debt? If So, How Do You Get Out?

You may be living the life of instant gratification and not be aware how it is affecting your personal wealth building goals. You probably buy impulsively more than you think. The easiest easy to find out is keep track of what you buy for a thirty-day period. You may find you have an 'want mentality'. We seem to focus on what we want instead of what we really need. The only way to break the instant gratification cycle is develop a 'need mentality' instead.

Look hard at your thirty-day purchases and highlight any frivolous spending you find. Add up all the frivolous spending and take that same amount, whether it is $10 or $100, and put it in a savings account or use it to pay down debt. Get into the mindset of asking yourself 'Do I really need it' before making any purchase at all. After a little practice, it will become second nature.

You will probably be surprised at how much extra money you have left in the bank at month end if you simply practice this approach.

Other Ways to Get Back on Track

If the current economic downturn has made you realize that you are one paycheck away from financial ruin, you can get back on track. Start practicing the following:

- Do I always feel as though I am behind in my work?
- Do I want myself and my team to be more productive?
- Do I need to find a balance between work and home?
- Do my team members shirk from responsibility?
- Do I struggle with distractions?

- Do I work for a business with frequent turnaround of employees?

Do You Have Too Much Debt?

Even though you might be getting by and are even able to save enough for a family vacation every few years you are probably carrying too much debt. How do you know? Some of the following will help you decide.

- The European countries involved in WWII were heavily in debt to the US.
- The US economy was very strong and the value of dollar had appreciated.
- Of all the major world currencies, only the US dollar was backed by gold.
- The US agreed to link the dollar to the gold price of $35 per ounce and exchange gold bullion for dollars.

This may sound elementary but the only way to get control of your personal finances is to save more, spend less and avoid bad debt. Money does matter and you will not be able to survive without it. You need to respect and manage your money before you will see a change in your finances.

Unlocking The Secrets of Creating Enlightened Wealth

Marc Victor Hansen, co-author of the *Chicken Soup for the Soul* books, and superstar financial advisor Robert G. Allen's "Cracking the Millionaire Code" is an illuminating book that presents a completely innovative outlook on both wealth and wealth creation, and unveils the secrets of successful wealth accumulation as it outshines traditional fiscal philosophy.

Some ideas presented in the book and illustrated at length include the concept that money is merely a representation of energy or the time invested by an individual to create something; that the more of it one has, the larger this representation becomes. Yet another is that money made through ethical means is both professionally *and* spiritually satisfying, and that is part of the path to true life happiness.

Impressions

For those looking to jump-start their own independent financial education, this is a great book to begin with. The premise of this book is that every one of us is fated for a more successful, copious life at this very moment, and that in order to unbridle this unlimited potential and make unimaginable wealth a reality each of us must find the way to "crack" our own wealth vault. The authors lay out a 101 day plan to aid readers in identifying and then "cracking" their own distinct millionaire code.

The structured architecture of the book is very helpful in aiding readers through the 101 days the plan spans. Throughout the plan, the authors provide helpful and stimulating questions with which to assistance readers through processing their own ideas as they likewise progress through the steps and chapters of the book. The high level of organization and well-defined stages make this book a great choice for expanding one's financial education.

Spirituality vs. Practicality

The authors realize that both business matters and creating wealth are practical, concrete subjects, but also recognize that there can be a more personal and spiritual side to these arenas as well. For instance, the authors pose that instead of the traditional business maxim "give and take" that the incredibly successful have an innovative spin on the aphorism, changing it to "give and give", which is the polar opposite of "take and take", the face of business and wealth-building that is unpopular.

Closely related to "give and give" is the concept of "enlightened wealth". In this idea, individuals create wealth in order to give it away to charity. This is a very noble idea, and both "give and give" and "enlightened wealth" are incredibly inspiring and honorable pursuits.

The part of "Cracking the Millionaire Code" that really is effective is that it requires action on the part of the reader; he or she cannot just read the book and then have their financial problems vanish spontaneously.

In order for the plan outlined in the book to work, the individual must take matters into his or her own hands, taking ownership and responsibility for their financial situation and making of it what they will.

Being inspired by another to make a change is a very powerful influence, as is the dawning realization that one can really have control over one's financial life; the control to make things better, to make things worse, to actually have an influence and be able to see the results. This, of course, is in direct opposition to the New Age tenet that individuals must merely open themselves up in order to receive the good and benefit that the universe has to offer. Allen and Hansen describe, in very clear and plain language, that in order to acquire and accumulate wealth, the individual **must** take action.

As previously mentioned, this book has a very preternatural tone to it, and for those who are not particularly spiritual, this may be a challenge to overcome. As long as one reads the entire text with an open mind, which should be done regardless in order to truly absorb and assimilate the information in order to decide whether or not it is worth implementation, this really should not be too much of a distraction.

The authors still present ideas, techniques, and other helpful information that can be easily implemented throughout life and business without the belief in a higher power. One such piece of tried-and-true advice is to build a solid support structure; surround yourself with family and friends who truly love you, care about you, and wish you to succeed. This is sound advice because if you were to surround yourself with people who belittled you and talked down to you, it would be very hard indeed to muster the courage, confidence, and belief in yourself that creating wealth requires.

Another great point the authors bring forth is that of joining forces with other individuals and companies in search of mutual profit, such as cross-promotional opportunities. This is a great solution for readers who feel stuck in their current situation and aren't really sure how exactly to get out of the rut; bringing new ideas and perspectives into the fold might be just the thing!

For those readers who *are* spiritual to any degree, it may be a bit easier to make the connection between the anecdotes in the text to the reader's individual life experiences, perhaps making the close reading of the book more intense. One of the major tenets that authors present to readers is a concept similar to "let go and let God" in that they urge readers, when things get too stressful or they feel they are unable to handle a specific situation, to seek the help of their higher power.

While this may seem an evasive move, it really encourages readers to take a step back, take a breath, take a break if possible, and clear their mind so that they can understand and analyze the problematic situation in a new way. Again, although presented in a spiritual way, this is a real-world solution that can be done without the belief in a higher power.

Either way, if readers are willing to expose themselves to and attempt to look at things from a new perspective, as is the true intent of the book, then they will absolutely receive the utmost benefit from it. After finishing it, if readers walk away with a sharper sense for and ability to spot ethical money generating opportunities, then they will have absolutely benefited from reading it.

Playtime, Anyone?

While packing readers brains with pragmatic business information, and opening their souls to possibility, Hansen and Allen also find room to help them think out of the box and "free their minds" with exercises nestled in each chapter. For instance, throughout the text there are word puzzles and codes that the reader can solve along the way to make sure their brains stay limber and open to new information.

In Closing

This book is thought-provoking and at times personally challenging. It does lay out an exact plan for readers to follow in order to crack their own code and reveal their true potential as well as help them actualize the fruits of putting that potential into action. It promotes many facets of not only a healthy financial position, but also fosters working towards a healthier life.

By writing a text which places emphasis on surrounding oneself with positive influences, working not only for oneself but also for the good of others, faith, charity, and honor, Allen and Hansen have put forth a very worthy compendium.

The 3 Step Process - From Debt to Start Building Wealth

If you are like all too many Americans, then you have as much or more debt than you do in actual assets. This is a position that will hold you back from becoming a wealthy person no matter how hard you try to get around it.

The good news for you is that there is an only three step process to go from being in debt to actually beginning to build wealth.

The following paragraphs go through these three steps in sufficient detail to teach you all that you need to know to get started in going from debt to wealth today.

Step 1 - Changing Your Mind-Set With Financial Education

Your mentality, mind set, and understanding is where you have to begin your journey from debt to wealth building. Educating yourself about the methods for getting out of debt is a critical first step.

There is a wealth of material written on this subject that plagues so many American consumers. Once you have learned the reasons that having this debt is holding you back from achieving your goals and dreams of building up wealth, you will be ready to learn more financial education about actually starting to build up wealth.

This can be accomplished in a wide variety of ways. Concepts of basic investing, using debt leverage to increase returns, and the concepts of passive investing all need to be learned. On top of this, your whole attitude towards money, spending, and investing needs to be changed, and this can all be accomplished through financial education.

It is not easy to move from a mind set of believing that it is better to spend money on short term pleasures and wants over to a mind set of understanding that you should save and invest as much as you possibly can.

Through financial education though, this can be accomplished. Do not be fooled into thinking that this involves reading a few short and quick articles. Changing your entire mindset where money is concerned is a titanic task that will require a good amount of continuing financial education over time.

Step 2 - Lowering Your Expenses Until You Achieve Positive Cash Flow

Getting out of debt and beginning to build up wealth does not happen as if by magic. It only happens when you actually manage to reduce your monthly expenses to the point that you have more money coming in than is going out of your accounts. Creating a budget is the first step to successfully accomplishing this. If you do not already have a budget, you need to create one right away.

Budgets are easy to set up. All that is required is a spreadsheet, or even a simple piece of paper. It should be divided into two columns. On the left side, you should title the heading income. Beneath this column you need to list all of the money that you have coming in consistently every month.

On the right side, you should title the heading expenses. Underneath this column, you must list out in detail all of the things on which you spend money.

It is helpful to be as specific as possible. Simply listing out a few generic headings like entertainment or utilities is not detailed enough. In order to reduce monthly expenses, you need to understand where your money is truly going, and what you are really spending it on.

As an example, simply showing entertainment and a number next to it will not tell you much. But if you break it down to Starbucks Coffee, and show that you are spending $20 or more a week on it, it will be easy to see a place where you can make a relatively painless cut of $80 per month by buying and brewing your coffee at home.

Similarly, if you show a utilities bill with a figure next to it, this will not help you to make any cuts. But when you show that you are spending from $80 to $100 per month on just cable entertainment, then you will see a way to take a Netflix membership instead and save $50 to $80 per month.

There are many ways to lower your monthly expenses until you create a positive cash flow. An often overlooked idea is to simply bundle your utilities together. By combining your telephone, Internet, television programing, and even cell phone providers into one single provider, you can lower these substantial bills by as much as forty or more percent per month. By switching one night out a week from dinner out to a pizza in or picnic in the park, you can save another significant amount per month.

Obtaining a positive cash flow will allow you to do several critical things. On the one hand, it will permit you to start aggressively paying down your debts. This should be done by paying all of the extra money that you have per month against the lowest balance bill first. Once this bill has been eliminated, the minimum payment that you were making on it can then be applied to the next lowest balance bill, and so on.

This creates a snowball effect that allows each bill to be paid down at a faster rate than the last one. One day you will wake up and discover that you have positive cash flow and no debt left.

Step 3 - Investing with the Goal of Capital Gains and Cash Flow

The third and most important step centers around investing proactively. This involves looking for investments that provide capital gains and cash flow. Simply saving money and putting it in the bank or into a low yield CD or treasury bond will not accomplish much. You need to seek out investments that will actually create a passive income. This is what the wealthy do consistently.

It is important for you to understand what the differences between these two concepts of capital gains in investments and cash flow in investments are so that you can properly seek out opportunities for smarter investing. Cash flow should be considered first and capital gains second in practically any investment.

Cash flow investing involves putting money into assets that literally return a small amount on the investment in question periodically, for the entire time that you have this investment. Cash flow investing revolves around holding on to the investment as a strategy. Income from cash flow investing is typically passive.

It is true that income that you receive from such cash flow investing can be in smaller amounts, but it is brought in on a routine and consistent basis. You keep this asset while you benefit from it financially. Given enough time, the entire return on investment that you get from this cash flow investing offers the potential to be far more significant than any single income that you get from a larger investment in which you employ a strategy of capital gains.

Capital Gains investing on the other hand, involves purchasing an investment at a low price with the intent of later selling it for a greater price. This difference in price represents your profit for investing your hard earned capital.

To profit from this strategy, you will have to sell your asset to capture the profit. This income amount that comes in is typically a larger amount received at one time. To keep investing with a capital gains strategy in mind, you will have to purchase another asset cheaply and sell it dearly.

Conclusion

Once you make the primary step and decide to change your mindset, new opportunities will show up in your world as a result of it. Use these new opportunities to learn and educate yourself and you are on your way to build wealth.

The 7 Best Practices
to Build Lasting Wealth in Your Life

Building wealth in your life is not a small or simple accomplishment. It takes real, hard work.

If you wish to become accomplished at building lasting wealth in your own life, then you will need to follow some sensible steps to achieve this.

The following paragraphs go through the seven best practices for effectively building up lasting wealth for yourself.

1. Understand that Money Is an Invention and Wealth is Real

When you are embarking on the journey to create lasting wealth in your life, you need to understand one important concept to begin. The wealth that you are looking to create is real. It exists in the form of investments, holdings, and assets such as stocks, bonds, real estate, gold and silver bullion, as well as in various other forms.

Money is an artificial concept that goes up and down in real worth and meaning. It was created to express values of wealth. Having a lot of money in the bank does not truly make you wealthy. Especially since 1971 all money is Fiat money and not backed up by gold or anything else.

It was no intrinsic value. Having a great amount of assets and holdings that furnish you with such money does make you wealthy. Money derives from wealth and not the other way around.

2. Focus on Contributing to Others

The people who have become the wealthiest in the world are those whose endeavors had them making the world a better place. The Henry Ford's and Thomas Edison's of our country made enormous impacts that are still presently felt and with us every time that you start up your car or turn on a light bulb with a switch.

It is in making a real contribution to other people and society in general that you create not only a meaningful life, but also great personal wealth over time. This is where your focus should be, on how you can improve the lives of other people through your efforts. Start with this, and the wealth will come as a reward for your accomplishments in bettering the world. As a side effect you will never be bored, depressed or lonely.

3. Understand Who You Are and What Your Passion Proves To Be

There is a wise saying regarding what you should do with your life. It is, "do what you love and the money will follow." Very few people achieve wealth through pursuing a business activity that they despise. It is instead the ones who follow their passions that are the most successful, both professionally and financially.

Colonel Sanders loved cooking and amazing chicken recipes. He followed his passion to create the world's largest and best known chicken restaurant franchise. Michael Dell loved computers and laptops.

His passion led him to create an enormous and well respected computer manufacturing business that is a household brand name to this day.

Steve Jobs knew early on that computers and electronics were his first love. As a result of following his passion, he created the Apple personal computer, iPod, iPhone, and iPad. When you find and follow your passion wholeheartedly, then you will see the wealth come along with it, though it may take some time.

4. Only Take A Job That Will Teach You - Start Your Own Business

When you are going to work for someone else, you should only do this if the job that they offer you can teach you something, preferably some valuable skill or ability that you could not easily internalize otherwise. When you reach the point working for someone that you can not learn anything else from them or the job, then you should look for another one that can teach you still more.

In life, you need to always be growing and learning in order to begin to achieve wealth building. You should also endeavor to start your own business when you come up with a truly wonderful idea. The vast majority of those who build up wealth do so working for themselves. There are many advantages to this, not the least of which are the tax advantages to running your own company.

5. Use Debt Leveraging to Invest and Build Up Passive Income

To create and build up significant wealth in your life, you are going to have to do more than simply save money and put it in the bank. You are going to have to master the concepts of using debt to leverage your investments and generating passive income.

A common way of using debt as a leverage to increase your investments is through purchasing properties with only a small amount of money down.

Your investment is able to gain a much larger percentage this way, since you have used another business or institution's capital in order to control this larger investment. As an example, when you buy a $100,000 house with only $10,000 down, you are using the power of leverage to control ten times the amount of asset that you contributed to the investment. When the investment gains ten percent, or ten thousand dollars, then you have realized a one hundred percent gain, and all through leveraging your money at a ten to one ratio.

Taking these houses and renting them out to tenants in exchange for monthly rental income is a form of building up passive income. The asset works for you to create additional streams of income, and you receive the money for simply owning the investment. There are many other forms of passive income that you can learn about and become involved in too. These regular forms of additional income are what separate the wealthy class from the rest of us.

6. Continue Educating Yourself on a Daily Basis

The worlds of finance and investment opportunities are changing around you literally every single day. Because of this, you can never be content with the knowledge base that you have built up for yourself.

You should always be reading articles, books, information, and informative websites that you can teach you about the various opportunities in which you can become involved.

Alternative energy such as solar and wind, and water desalination plants and the companies that build and install them, are a few examples of new trends that can provide you with tremendous opportunities.

If you are not constantly reading about them, they will pass you by, or you will hear about them once everyone else is aware of them and the magical ground floor opportunity is long gone. There is nothing worse than saying to yourself, "If only I had known about this technology and its opportunity sooner."

7. Get A Mentor for Yourself - Wealthy Entrepreneurs Make the Best Ones

If you can get a really good mentor to help shepherd you along in the ways of building up wealth and creating success, then you will be better off by far. Successful entrepreneurs make the best such mentors for you. They can be found by joining business organizations and clubs, or through other networks.

Other people will mentor you as a for pay service, to share their considerable accomplishments with you as well as their advice for your personal situation. Having a person who has successfully achieved wealth and great success to guide you along in your own journey is like having a coach or trainer on your personal team that gets phenomenal results. Reading and learning for yourself is good and should not be neglected, but having your own personal mentor is the best possible scenario.

<u>RESOURCES</u>

"Free Bonus Content"

For additional 'Wealth Advisor' editions please go to amazon.com.

If you have additional interest in preserving your wealth and invest in silver please also check out the author's book: 'Building Wealth with Silver', which is available at amazon.

Building Wealth with Silver Book:
www.buildingwealthwithsilver.com

Resources

Thomas Herold, Author

Thomas Herold is a successful entrepreneur and personal development coach. After a career with one of the largest electronic companies in the world, he realized that a regular job would never fully satisfy his need for connection on a deep level.

The only way to live his full potential was to start building his own business and find new ways to be in service to others.

For over 25 years he has helped many people – including himself – build their dream businesses. Toward that goal, he focuses on education – simplified and enhanced by modern technology. He is the author of three books with over 200,000 copies distributed worldwide.

Other than his passion for creating businesses, Thomas has spent over 20 years in the self-development field. Placing emphasis on the exploration of consciousness and building practical applications that allow people to express their purpose and passion in life, Thomas's work in this area has provided ample and happy proof that this approach works.

He believes that every person has at least one gift and that, when this gift is developed and nourished, it will serve as a fountainhead of personal happiness and help contribute to a better, more sustainable world.

For the past seven years Thomas Herold has studied the monetary system and has experienced some profound insights on how money and wealth are related.

Thomas's ultimate vision for the Wealth Advisor is to empower people to adopt a wealthy mindset and to create abundance for themselves and others. His ability to explain complex information in simple terms makes him an outstanding teacher and coach.